LIVING  LITURGY™

for Extraordinary Ministers of Holy Communion

Year C • 2019

Brian Schmisek
Katy Beedle Rice
Diana Macalintal

LITURGICAL PRESS
Collegeville, Minnesota
www.litpress.org

Cover design by Monica Bokinskie. Art by Deborah Luke (pages 6–14, 58–60, 100–126), Tanja Butler (cover and pages 16–24, 40–54, 82–98), and Ned Bustard (pages 26–38, 62–80, 128–42).

ISSN 1933-3129

ISBN 978-0-8146-4523-9   ISBN 978-0-8146-4547-5 (ebook)

Presented to

_____

*in grateful appreciation
for ministering as an
Extraordinary Minister
of
Holy Communion*

_____

_____

(date)

Extraordinary typically refers to outstanding or exceptional. But extraordinary ministers of Holy Communion are "extra"-ordinary in the sense of "in addition to" the ordinary (as well as being outstanding and exceptional!). Ordinary ministers of Holy Communion are the ordained and those properly installed as acolytes, usually seminarians. In parishes today there are simply not enough "ordinary" ministers of Holy Communion, so we call forth additional ministers, referred to as "extraordinary." Imagine how long the distribution of Communion would take if the ordained or seminarians were the only ones who distributed! It is not only because of need, however, that we have extraordinary ministers of Holy Communion. It is also by virtue of one's baptism. We parishioners are grateful that so many baptized Christians respond to the call to serve as extraordinary ministers of Holy Communion. In so doing we are reminded that we are all holy, and we are all called to ministry by virtue of our Christian baptism.

Preparing for This Ministry

Though different dioceses and parishes have slightly different preparation requirements for those who would be extraordinary ministers of Holy Communion, there is preparation nonetheless. We hope that this book will be a source of reflection for such preparation, and also for ongoing reflection throughout one's ministry. We know that it is not enough to simply attend a training event and never look back. Each ministry of the church requires regular prayer, reflection, reading, and thoughtfulness. This book is intended to assist with that process by providing prayers and reflection for each Sunday and for certain solemnities. This resource can also be used by groups who would like to share their faith with questions that prompt discussion.

Holy Communion for the Homebound and Sick

In the New Testament Letter of James we learn about the concern and care that the early Christians had for those members of their community who were sick. Such care and concern was a hallmark of Jesus' own ministry, and it has been a Christian charism ever since. Each week there are parishioners who are not able to join us for the liturgy, and so the Eucharist is brought to them as a sign of our unity. Extraordinary ministers of Holy Communion are often those who perform this ministry, and, in so doing, they extend the parish's reach to so many more fellow parishioners. This book is intended to be a resource for them as well.

Adapting This Resource for
Holy Communion for the Homebound and Sick

The Communion rite (Ordinary Rite of Communion of the Sick) is provided as a separate publication to this book and enclosed within. Those who are extraordinary ministers of Holy Communion have undoubtedly been made familiar with this rite as part of their preparation. This book may be adapted for use with the rite, by sharing the gospel reflection, the prayers, or even the reflection question, so that the visit becomes a true ministry. It is to be remembered that ministers are not mere functionaries. As such, extraordinary ministers of Holy Communion bring not only the presence of Christ in the eucharistic species, but the presence of Christ in their very person by virtue of their baptism. So this book has been designed with that in mind, and it can be used to assist with making this a meaningful encounter and ministry.

In today's gospel Jesus speaks of the coming of the Son of Man. As we begin a new church year, let us ask for God's mercy and forgiveness, so as to be ready to greet Jesus when he comes again . . .

Prayer

To you, O Lord, we lift up our voices. Our souls proclaim your praise, for you guide us in your truth and teach us your paths. We lift up our voices in praise.

Show us, Lord, your love, *and grant us your salvation.* **Amen.**

Gospel   Luke 21:25-28, 34-36

Jesus said to his disciples: "There will be signs in the sun, the moon, and the stars, and on earth nations will be in dismay, perplexed by the roaring of the sea and the waves. People will die of fright in anticipation of what is coming upon the world, for the powers of the heavens will be shaken. And then they will see the Son of Man coming in a cloud with power and great glory. But when these signs begin to happen, stand erect and raise your heads because your redemption is at hand.

"Beware that your hearts do not become drowsy from carousing and drunkenness and the anxieties of daily life, and that day catch you by surprise like a trap. For that day will assault everyone who lives on the face of the earth. Be vigilant at all times and pray that you have the strength to escape the tribulations that are imminent and to stand before the Son of Man."

Brief Silence

For Reflection

The gospel reading for today gives the reader signs that will accompany the end times, the coming of the Son of Man. But we would be mistaken if we took these passages literally. And it's certainly true that hundreds if not thousands of people have done just that—looked for these signs to be fulfilled literally.

The message of this passage sought to give hope to a beleaguered people, the Christians, who anticipated their redemption. Many of them desperately wanted to see the coming of the Son of Man who would establish justice and peace. Many of the early Christians were on the bottom of the social ladder, experiencing tribulations and trials. Jesus himself had faced a violent end at the hands of the state. The Christians needed to be reminded that their salvation would come, and that they also needed to be vigilant, watching for that same salvation. And at the time this gospel was written there were many other Christians who may have lost hope or grown weary of waiting. This message was for them; and the message is also for us.

✦ As Christians living in the year 2018 we realize that our own personal end will likely come before the second coming of Jesus. Thinking about your own mortality, how would you live this coming year if you knew it was your last on earth?

Brief Silence

Prayer

Good and gracious God, we come before you mindful of our limited time on this earth. Give us the sense to live each day with meaning and purpose, striving to do your will. May we feed the hungry, clothe the naked, and give drink to the thirsty, knowing we are serving you. We ask this through Christ our Lord. **Amen.**

THE IMMACULATE CONCEPTION OF THE BLESSED VIRGIN MARY

In today's second reading we hear that we have been chosen before the foundation of the world to be holy and without blemish before God. Let us pause to ask for God's mercy and pardon for the times we have not lived up to this call . . .

Prayer

You have blessed all creation, Lord, with the gift of Mary, prepared from birth to trust in you and proclaim your Word. May her song of justice be ever on our lips.

Sing joyfully to the Lord, all you lands; *break into song; sing praise.* **Amen.**

Gospel Luke 1:26-38

The angel Gabriel was sent from God to a town of Galilee called Nazareth, to a virgin betrothed to a man named Joseph, of the house of David, and the virgin's name was Mary. And coming to her, he said, "Hail, full of grace! The Lord is with you." But she was greatly troubled at what was said and pondered what sort of greeting this might be. Then the angel said to her, "Do not be afraid, Mary, for you have found favor with God. Behold, you will conceive in your womb and bear a son, and you shall name him Jesus. He will be great and will be called Son of the Most High, and the Lord God will give him the throne of David his father, and he will rule over the house of Jacob forever, and of his Kingdom there will be no end." But Mary said to the angel, "How can this be, since I have no relations with a man?" And the angel said to her in reply, "The Holy Spirit will come upon you, and the power of the Most High will overshadow you. Therefore the child to be born will be called holy, the Son of God. And behold, Elizabeth, your relative, has also conceived a son in her old age, and this is the sixth month for her who was called barren; for nothing will be impossible for God." Mary said, "Behold, I am the handmaid of the Lord. May it be done to me according to your word." Then the angel departed from her.

Brief Silence

For Reflection
The immaculate conception is a difficult concept for adults to grasp, much less children. Though it is a basic element of faith, it is the source of never-ending confusion and much explanatory catechesis. Frankly, the issue is not made easier when the reading for this solemnity narrates the conception of Jesus (also known as the annunciation) and not the immaculate conception (the conception of Mary). But as we know, there is no scriptural passage that narrates the conception of Mary, so the church gives us the story about the conception of Jesus! No wonder confusion abounds.

We recall that every Marian title ultimately says more about Jesus than it does about Mary. And that is certainly true with the immaculate conception, which claims that the salvific effects of what God has done in Christ preserved Mary from sin from the moment of her conception. We can understand and appreciate some confusion regarding the meaning of this feast, which celebrates Mary's immaculate character from the moment of conception, by reading from the gospel about the conception of Jesus by Mary's own word of *fiat*.

✦ As God protected Mary from sin from the moment of her conception, he also desires to wash all sin from us. What spiritual and sacramental practices reveal God's forgiveness to you?

Brief Silence

Prayer
Lord, Jesus Christ, your mother was immaculate from the moment of her conception. Her freedom to do the will of God was expressed in her *fiat*, and lived throughout her life. Give us the same freedom to respond generously to the call of God in our own lives, so that we may do your will. We ask this in your name, for you live and reign with the Father and the Spirit. **Amen.**

In today's gospel John the Baptist proclaims a baptism of repentance for the forgiveness of sins. For the areas in our own lives crying for repentance and forgiveness, we ask for God's mercy . . .

Prayer

You, O God, chose John to be your voice crying out in the desert. This Advent, may our voices join with his to announce your salvation to all the world.

The Lord has done great things for us, *we are glad indeed.* **Amen.**

Gospel   Luke 3:1-6

In the fifteenth year of the reign of Tiberius Caesar, when Pontius Pilate was governor of Judea, and Herod was tetrarch of Galilee, and his brother Philip tetrarch of the region of Ituraea and Trachonitis, and Lysanias was tetrarch of Abilene, during the high priesthood of Annas and Caiaphas, the word of God came to John the son of Zechariah in the desert. John went throughout the whole region of the Jordan, proclaiming a baptism of repentance for the forgiveness of sins, as it is written in the book of the words of the prophet Isaiah: / *A voice of one crying out in the desert:* / *"Prepare the way of the Lord,* / *make straight his paths. / Every valley shall be filled / and every mountain and hill shall be made low. / The winding roads shall be made straight, / and the rough ways made smooth, / and all flesh shall see the salvation of God."*

Brief Silence

For Reflection

After his introductory material, including the infancy narratives in chapters 1 and 2, Luke picks up the gospel story he inherited from Mark. That is, today's reading from Luke is based on the opening verses of the Gospel of Mark with important additions. Beginning with John the Baptist's preaching, Luke situates the Christ-event in a particular historical time and place, for, as he tells us in Acts 26:26, these things did not happen in a corner. And it is precisely because of Luke's desire to give us the historical details that scholars can be fairly confident of their dating. Luke cites both civil and religious leaders to situate the Christ-event in history.

The historical details do much for the modern Christian (and ancient Christian for that matter) in demonstrating that Jesus was a historical figure. The Christ-event is not a mere myth like so many other Greek and Roman tales. Jesus was a living, breathing Jewish human being who lived in the Roman Empire in the province of Judea. Luke is a gifted storyteller, theologian, and evangelist. We do well to read his story carefully.

✦ As a parish how might you prepare to welcome with love and joy the people who will join your community to celebrate Christmas?

Brief Silence

Prayer

Lord, God Almighty, you have done great things for us and we are blessed. May we share with all peoples the good news of what you have done, reflecting the goodness and mercy you have to offer, so that we are true exemplars of your Christ. We ask this in his name. **Amen.**

On this Gaudete Sunday, we are reminded to rejoice always in the Lord. As we prepare to enter into this celebration, we reflect on how we have lived this call to joy . . .

Prayer

You anoint us with your Spirit, O Lord, that we may bring glad tidings. Let the song of joy we sing this day be lived in our lives.

Sing praise to the Lord and shout with joy, *for God is in our midst, the Holy One of Israel.* **Amen.**

Gospel   **Luke 3:10-18**

The crowds asked John the Baptist, "What should we do?" He said to them in reply, "Whoever has two cloaks should share with the person who has none. And whoever has food should do likewise." Even tax collectors came to be baptized and they said to him, "Teacher, what should we do?" He answered them, "Stop collecting more than what is prescribed." Soldiers also asked him, "And what is it that we should do?" He told them, "Do not practice extortion, do not falsely accuse anyone, and be satisfied with your wages."

Now the people were filled with expectation, and all were asking in their hearts whether John might be the Christ. John answered them all, saying, "I am baptizing you with water, but one mightier than I is coming. I am not worthy to loosen the thongs of his sandals. He will baptize you with the Holy Spirit and fire. His winnowing fan is in his hand to clear his threshing floor and to gather the wheat into his barn, but the chaff he will burn with unquenchable fire." Exhorting them in many other ways, he preached good news to the people.

Brief Silence

For Reflection

We hear the preaching of John the Baptist today. We are moving toward the imminent coming of the Son of Man. John would have been a fine preacher of the fire and brimstone variety, motivating his audience to action. Three times different groups ask him, "What should we do?" And three times John has an answer founded in justice and mercy. Follow the rules; share with those who have not. This is fairly simple and straightforward advice. And because of it he was thought to be the Messiah.

We can almost feel the crowd's anticipation and excitement. Here is someone who is preaching justice and mercy. Furthermore, John tells them that this is only the beginning. Another is coming. John speaks to them of an unquenchable fire, which seems a distant image from the "lilies of the field" Jesus that Luke will narrate later in his gospel. John's own expectation of a Messiah who would bring judgment, wrath, and an "unquenchable fire" might not have been met by Jesus. John would not be the first to have dashed expectations and hopes. Jesus has another way. Still, John's essential message of practicing justice and mercy are good ways to prepare for Christ's coming.

✦ In today's gospel the people ask John the Baptist, "What should we do?" As you enter into the final nine days of Advent what is one action you might take to serve Jesus' mission of mercy and justice?

Brief Silence

Prayer

O God, you are the source of all joy. In your Christ your love for the world is enfleshed. Animate us with your spirit so that we may be doers of the word, practicing justice and mercy to all those we encounter. We ask this in the name of your Son our Lord, Jesus Christ. **Amen.**

In today's gospel Elizabeth tells Mary, "Blessed are you who believed that what was spoken to you by the Lord would be fulfilled." Let us prepare to enter into this liturgy by opening ourselves up to the transformative word of God . . .

Prayer

Grant us, Lord, Mary's faith to trust your word, Elizabeth's hope to hear your voice, and John's delight to sing your joy that our hearts may be ready to receive you.

Turn our faces to see your glory *so we may dwell in your salvation's light.* **Amen.**

Gospel　　　　　　　　　　　　　　　　　　　　**Luke 1:39-45**

Mary set out and traveled to the hill country in haste to a town of Judah, where she entered the house of Zechariah and greeted Elizabeth. When Elizabeth heard Mary's greeting, the infant leaped in her womb, and Elizabeth, filled with the Holy Spirit, cried out in a loud voice and said, "Blessed are you among women, and blessed is the fruit of your womb. And how does this happen to me, that the mother of my Lord should come to me? For at the moment the sound of your greeting reached my ears, the infant in my womb leaped for joy. Blessed are you who believed that what was spoken to you by the Lord would be fulfilled."

Brief Silence

For Reflection

This Advent season is especially short and can make for a hectic, frenetic pace as we consider all that needs to happen before the holiday. Some are preparing homes to receive guests, others are preparing meals, and many are doing both! Still others are setting out on their travels to see loved ones during these holy days. We are busy with many tasks.

We might imagine Mary and Elizabeth sharing these feelings in this reading from Luke. Mary visits her cousin and Elizabeth has certainly been preparing for her guest. The greeting is joyful and Luke tells us that Elizabeth was filled with the Holy Spirit.

This gospel passage calls to mind for us how important human relationships are. Amidst all the travel, preparation, meals, and general business, the bonds of human love bind us together. When we consider the holiday season with its pressing demands let us recall the ultimate reason for our cares and concerns. We have in mind those we love and care for. May the relationships we celebrate this season, especially the relationships we have in Christ, inspire us to live in a meaningful way.

✦ Mary and Elizabeth share each other's joy and offer strength to one another in their pregnancies. In our spiritual life we need companions who can point out where God is working in our lives. Other times we are called to be the one who bears witness to Christ's presence in another. How might we cultivate these spiritual friendships?

Brief Silence

Prayer

Lord Jesus Christ, as one who lived among us you know the power and meaning of human relationships. May our loved ones know the care and concern we have for them, by our living lives of authenticity and transparency. We ask this in your holy name. **Amen.**

We gather to celebrate the birth of Emmanuel, God with us, now and forever. As we prepare to enter into the mystery of the incarnation let us pause to ask for pardon and healing . . .

Prayer

In every age, through sinner and saint, in our darkest nights and days of peace, you have made us, Lord, your lineage of grace.

For this may we never be silent. *Forever let us sing of your goodness, O God.* **Amen.**

Gospel   **Luke 2:1-14 (Mass at Midnight)**

In those days a decree went out from Caesar Augustus that the whole world should be enrolled. This was the first enrollment, when Quirinius was governor of Syria. So all went to be enrolled, each to his own town. And Joseph too went up from Galilee from the town of Nazareth to Judea, to the city of David that is called Bethlehem, because he was of the house and family of David, to be enrolled with Mary, his betrothed, who was with child. While they were there, the time came for her to have her child, and she gave birth to her firstborn son. She wrapped him in swaddling clothes and laid him in a manger, because there was no room for them in the inn.

Now there were shepherds in that region living in the fields and keeping the night watch over their flock. The angel of the Lord appeared to them and the glory of the Lord shone around them, and they were struck with great fear. The angel said to them, "Do not be afraid; for behold, I proclaim to you good news of great joy that will be for all the people. For today in the city of David a savior has been born for you who is Christ and Lord. And this will be a sign for you: you will find an infant wrapped in swaddling clothes and lying in a manger." And suddenly there was a multitude of the heavenly host with the angel, praising God and saying: / "Glory to God in the highest / and on earth peace to those on whom his favor rests."

Brief Silence

For Reflection

This gospel relates the scene we connect most readily with Christmas. Jesus, Son of God and son of Mary, is born in Bethlehem but since there is no room at the inn he has no cradle for a bed. Instead, a feedbox becomes his resting place. We've pictured this scene so many times that maybe it has stopped shocking us. It certainly would have shocked Jesus' first visitors. This baby, whose birth is proclaimed by an angel, is to be found with his mother and father sleeping among the animals. This one, whom the shepherds are told is "Savior," "Messiah," and "Lord," enters the world as a helpless baby who must depend on others for all of his physical needs. That God chose to become a human being is remarkable, but that God chose to become a human being born in a barn to poor parents is even more so. This child of whom angels sing is born into the messiness of human life. Can we also find him there?

✦ The angel of the Lord tells the shepherds that the birth of Jesus is good news of great joy for all people. How do you invite others, especially those who might not share your faith, to enter into this joy?

Brief Silence

Prayer

Lord Jesus Christ, you are the hope of the world. Your life gives light to all. May our lives reflect the hope, light, and peace you bring, so that we may all live in harmony, as you desire. We ask this in your name for you live and reign with the Father and Spirit. **Amen.**

THE HOLY FAMILY OF JESUS, MARY, AND JOSEPH

Today we celebrate the Holy Family of Jesus, Mary, and Joseph. We also remember that we are children of God and therefore members of God's family. For the times that have not lived up to this identity, we ask for pardon and healing . . .

Prayer

With a father's love and a mother's tender care, you have called us your children, O God. Help us to live lives worthy of the name of Christ.

In our Father's house we sing God's praise. *Blessed are they God has chosen to be his own.* **Amen.**

Gospel   Luke 2:41-52

Each year Jesus' parents went to Jerusalem for the feast of Passover, and when he was twelve years old, they went up according to festival custom. After they had completed its days, as they were returning, the boy Jesus remained behind in Jerusalem, but his parents did not know it. Thinking that he was in the caravan, they journeyed for a day and looked for him among their relatives and acquaintances, but not finding him, they returned to Jerusalem to look for him. After three days they found him in the temple, sitting in the midst of the teachers, listening to them and asking them questions, and all who heard him were astounded at his understanding and his answers. When his parents saw him, they were astonished, and his mother said to him, "Son, why have you done this to us? Your father and I have been looking for you with great anxiety." And he said to them, "Why were you looking for me? Did you not know that I must be in my Father's house?" But they did not understand what he said to them. He went down with them and came to Nazareth, and was obedient to them; and his mother kept all these things in her heart. And Jesus advanced in wisdom and age and favor before God and man.

Brief Silence

For Reflection

A missing child is a parent's worst fear. We might have been relying on someone else to keep an eye on this young one, only to realize that was a misunderstanding. Such things happen occasionally and often the child is found shortly thereafter. Other times it results in tragedy. But in today's gospel story the Holy Family had lost Jesus in the capital city of Jerusalem! This is a reminder that though Jesus' family is holy it was not without challenges, like any family. Joseph and Mary dealt with parenting a preteen who thought he was fine on his own. Obviously miscommunication was a challenge for them as it might be for us as well.

We recognize that family life can be messy, punctuated with misunderstandings, miscommunication, and mistakes. Such events are not "sinful" and they were obviously part of life for the Holy Family. Our own families are places of sanctity. We will have challenges as the Holy Family did. But we can deal with them forthrightly, knowing that the relationships we have in this most basic human unit are a means of sanctification.

✦ How does your family support each other in times of stress and sadness?

Brief Silence

Prayer

Spirit of God, you bind us together in bonds of love, friendship, and family. By these relationships we are sanctified for service. May we be reminded that these are holy bonds, even when they are stretched and stressed. Give us the wisdom and strength to support one another in good and challenging times. **Amen.**

As we gather today to consecrate this New Year to God through the intercession of Mary, the Holy Mother of God, let us pause to acknowledge our own sinfulness and need of God's mercy . . .

Prayer

As we enter a New Year of grace, O Lord, help us be present, like Mary, to all the blessings that you have prepared for your people.

Bless us, O God, in your mercy; *let all that has breath praise your holy name!* **Amen.**

Gospel   **Luke 2:16-21**

The shepherds went in haste to Bethlehem and found Mary and Joseph, and the infant lying in the manger. When they saw this, they made known the message that had been told them about this child. All who heard it were amazed by what had been told them by the shepherds. And Mary kept all these things, reflecting on them in her heart. Then the shepherds returned, glorifying and praising God for all they had heard and seen, just as it had been told to them.

When eight days were completed for his circumcision, he was named Jesus, the name given him by the angel before he was conceived in the womb.

Brief Silence

For Reflection

Catholics are known for having a devotion to Mary, the mother of Jesus. In many RCIA classes the topic of Mary consumes a great deal of the room's oxygen. Mary's role is also a flashpoint in discussions between Catholics and other Christians, especially Protestants. On its face such a title, Mother of God, can be perplexing. How can God, who exists from all eternity, have a mother? Where is that in the Scriptures? Of course, the statement says more about Jesus, who is the enfleshment (incarnation) of the Word of God.

But it would be too easy to become caught up in this Marian title as another example of outsized Catholic devotion to Mary. Instead, this title has its roots in the fifth century, one thousand years before Catholics and Protestants. And the claim is simply and profoundly this: that Jesus was the incarnation of God from the moment of his conception so that Mary can rightly be said to have borne the divine. Christianity is an incarnational faith. It is not that humanity must raise itself up to divinity, but rather, divinity humbles itself and enters into humanity.

✦ What are the ways you encounter the incarnational aspect of faith?

Brief Silence

Prayer

Lord, Jesus Christ, you were born of an earthly woman, thereby sanctifying and divinizing all of humanity. May we recognize the sanctity of all human life regardless of age, ethnicity, creed, or nationality, so that with this awareness we may become more like you, who loves without distinction. We ask this in your name. **Amen.**

On this great feast of Epiphany we are invited anew to walk in the light of the Lord. Let us seek God's mercy for the times we have preferred the darkness to this saving light . . .

Prayer

Where darkness covers the earth, your glory, O Lord, shines. Where nations rage in fear, your star lights the way to peace. Help us always to follow where you lead.

All you nations, raise your eyes and see: *Our God has come to save us.* **Amen.**

Gospel	Matt 2:1-12

When Jesus was born in Bethlehem of Judea, in the days of King Herod, behold, magi from the east arrived in Jerusalem, saying, "Where is the newborn king of the Jews? We saw his star at its rising and have come to do him homage." When King Herod heard this, he was greatly troubled, and all Jerusalem with him. Assembling all the chief priests and the scribes of the people, he inquired of them where the Christ was to be born. They said to him, "In Bethlehem of Judea, for thus it has been written through the prophet: / *And you, Bethlehem, land of Judah, / are by no means least among the rulers of Judah; / since from you shall come a ruler, / who is to shepherd my people Israel." /* Then Herod called the magi secretly and ascertained from them the time of the star's appearance. He sent them to Bethlehem and said, "Go and search diligently for the child. When you have found him, bring me word, that I too may go and do him homage." After their audience with the king they set out. And behold, the star that they had seen at its rising preceded them, until it came and stopped over the place where the child was. They were overjoyed at seeing the star, and on entering the house they saw the child with Mary his mother. They prostrated themselves and did him homage. Then they opened their treasures and offered him gifts of gold, frankincense, and myrrh. And having been warned in a dream not to return to Herod, they departed for their country by another way.

Brief Silence

For Reflection

The feast of the Epiphany is celebrated in many cultures and oftentimes more prominently than Christmas! At a time when many homes have taken down decorations and put away special dishes from the season, we are reminded that there are still celebrations to be had. This story of the visit from the magi is unique to Matthew's gospel and when read on its own terms it can be especially revealing. Often, however, we read this gospel with pre-conceived notions. For example, the text doesn't say how many magi there were but because they gave three gifts (gold, frankincense, and myrrh) artists, preachers, and homilists through the centuries talk about there being three kings. But even the term, "king," is not used in the gospel text. Instead, the term is "magi," which designated the Persian (modern-day Iran) priestly caste. Thus, Matthew foreshadows the post-resurrection mission to the Gentiles by showing Gentiles (Persians) coming to worship the child Jesus. Ultimately, this is a story about who Jesus is and what his mission will be. Salvation knows no bounds. This is a cause for celebration indeed!

✦ The magi follow a star that leads them to Jesus, God with us. In your life, how has creation helped you to know God?

Brief Silence

Prayer

Jesus Christ, our brother and Lord, your birth was made known by a sign in the heavens, and outsiders were the first to recognize this sign and worship you. Give us a spirit of wonder and openness to see signs of your presence too. Grant us hearts wide open to any and all who come to you and worship you. **Amen.**

On this feast of the Baptism of the Lord we recall the grace of our own baptism. As we are sprinkled with holy water let us prepare ourselves to enter into this celebration with joy and a renewed commitment to our own baptismal promises . . .

Prayer

From the light of the star, your grace appeared and now is revealed in the waters of baptism. In Christ your Son, may we ever be pleasing in your sight.

All you children of God, give glory to the Lord! *By our lives, let us glorify God.* **Amen.**

Gospel   **Luke 3:15-16, 21-22**

The people were filled with expectation, and all were asking in their hearts whether John might be the Christ. John answered them all, saying, "I am baptizing you with water, but one mightier than I is coming. I am not worthy to loosen the thongs of his sandals. He will baptize you with the Holy Spirit and fire."

After all the people had been baptized and Jesus also had been baptized and was praying, heaven was opened and the Holy Spirit descended upon him in bodily form like a dove. And a voice came from heaven, "You are my beloved Son; with you I am well pleased."

Brief Silence

For Reflection

The baptism of an infant is the cause of much joy, celebration, and love among family and friends. The baby is welcomed into the

Christian community, a community of grace, support, and encouragement in the face of all that life can bring. This ritual action has its roots not only in Jesus, but in John, "the Baptist" who was so named precisely because of this action he performed at the Jordan River.

As indicated by the gospels, the ministry of Jesus began at or shortly after his baptism. And Luke shows that the Holy Spirit was active at this time, descending upon Jesus "in bodily form like a dove." Further, Luke is also the only evangelist to say that Jesus was at prayer during this event. Luke shows Jesus at prayer more than any other evangelist. Luke will also show the early Christian community at prayer in the Acts of the Apostles.

May our prayer life, like that of Jesus, also be animated by the Holy Spirit, not only at moments of joy, but also in times of new beginnings.

✦ How is your prayer life animated by the Holy Spirit?

Brief Silence

Prayer

Spirit of God, you wash away sins with the waters of baptism and make a people for yourself. Give us the same spirit of openness, inclusion, and welcome so that we may draw more people to Christ by living lives of service and other-centeredness. We ask this in the name of Jesus, who underwent baptism himself. **Amen.**

In today's gospel reading Mary instructs the servers at the wedding feast in Cana, "Do whatever he tells you." These words are addressed to us as well in the life of faith. For the times that we have not listened attentively to the voice of Jesus calling us to righteousness, we ask for God's pardon and healing . . .

Prayer

By star and by water your glory has shone, and now at this feast of bridegroom and bride, your love is revealed by miraculous sign.

May we ever proclaim God's marvelous deeds *and sing of God's glory over all the earth.* **Amen.**

Gospel   John 2:1-11

There was a wedding at Cana in Galilee, and the mother of Jesus was there. Jesus and his disciples were also invited to the wedding. When the wine ran short, the mother of Jesus said to him, "They have no wine." And Jesus said to her, "Woman, how does your concern affect me? My hour has not yet come." His mother said to the servers, "Do whatever he tells you." Now there were six stone water jars there for Jewish ceremonial washings, each holding twenty to thirty gallons. Jesus told them, "Fill the jars with water." So they filled them to the brim. Then he told them, "Draw some out now and take it to the headwaiter." So they took it. And when the headwaiter tasted the water that had become wine, without knowing where it came from—although the servers who had drawn the water knew—, the headwaiter called the bridegroom and said to him, "Everyone serves good wine first, and then when people have drunk freely, an inferior one; but you have kept the good wine until now." Jesus did this as the beginning of his signs at Cana in Galilee and so revealed his glory, and his disciples began to believe in him.

Brief Silence

For Reflection

Although liturgically we are in Cycle C when we read from the Gospel of Luke, we begin Ordinary Time with this reading from the Gospel of John, which does not refer to Jesus' mother by name, for she is never named in this gospel, but rather, Mary is called "the mother of Jesus." According to this gospel, not only is she present at the beginning of Jesus' ministry, but she will be present at the cross too, accompanied by the Beloved Disciple (who, like the mother of Jesus, remains nameless). For the Gospel of John, the emphasis is on Jesus to such a degree that many other characters do not even have names!

And this is a good point for us. Namely, our emphasis should be on Jesus and his true identity. It is easy to be drawn away from him and look to novelties or curiosities. The Fourth Gospel reveals Jesus' identity as Son of God, the Word made flesh. We need look no further. For the disciple, and certainly for the evangelist, the focus is on Jesus for he is the incarnation of the Word of God and his words are life eternal.

✦ Jesus' signs disclose himself and the kingdom of God to us. What does today's gospel about the wedding feast in Cana reveal to you about Jesus?

Brief Silence

Prayer

Lord, God Almighty, you sent your Son into the world as the incarnation of your Word. His identity was disclosed by the signs he performed. Give us the wisdom and insight to perceive the signs of your word in our midst today. May we have the strength to follow your Son wherever he may lead. We ask this in his name, who lives and reigns with you and the spirit, one God forever and ever. **Amen.**

In today's second reading the apostle Paul tells us we are all members of Christ's body. For the times we have not acted in a way to befitting of the body of Christ we ask for pardon and forgiveness . . .

Prayer

You have fulfilled your Word in Christ, O God, and anointed us with his Spirit of life. With him, may we always bear glad tidings to those in need.

Today is holy to the Lord, our God. *Let us rejoice in God our savior.* **Amen.**

Gospel   Luke 1:1-4; 4:14-21

Since many have undertaken to compile a narrative of the events that have been fulfilled among us, just as those who were eyewitnesses from the beginning and ministers of the word have handed them down to us, I too have decided, after investigating everything accurately anew, to write it down in an orderly sequence for you, most excellent Theophilus, so that you may realize the certainty of the teachings you have received.

Jesus returned to Galilee in the power of the Spirit, and news of him spread throughout the whole region. He taught in their synagogues and was praised by all.

He came to Nazareth, where he had grown up, and went according to his custom into the synagogue on the sabbath day. He stood up to read and was handed a scroll of the prophet Isaiah. He unrolled the scroll and found the passage where it was written: / *The Spirit of the Lord is upon me, / because he has anointed me / to bring glad tidings to the poor. / He has sent me to proclaim liberty to captives / and recovery of sight to the blind, / to let the oppressed go free, / and to proclaim a year acceptable to the Lord. /*

Rolling up the scroll, he handed it back to the attendant and sat down, and the eyes of all in the synagogue looked intently at him. He said to them, "Today this Scripture passage is fulfilled in your hearing."

Brief Silence

For Reflection

There are many things to note in this brief opening to Luke's gospel, but it is significant that Luke says he is relying on the eyewitness of others, and thereby indicates that he was not an eyewitness himself. He is at least a second-generation Christian, who has looked into this story and told it so the believer Theophilus (the name means "God-lover") might have surety. By this emphasis on surety, even the modern reader recognizes that the story of Jesus is no mere myth. The events of Jesus' life, death, and resurrection really and truly happened.

But the church is not content to give us only the first four verses of the gospel on this Sunday. The second significant item to note is that we also read about Jesus' preaching in the synagogue at Nazareth in chapter 4. Jesus reads from the prophet and proclaims that the message is fulfilled in their midst. Jesus causes the blind to see and proclaims glad tidings to the poor. In so doing, he is the fulfillment of the hopes and expectations of the prophets, for the Spirit of the Lord is upon him.

✦ Jesus tells the people, "Today this Scripture passage is fulfilled in your hearing." How have you experienced the word of God being fulfilled in your own life?

Brief Silence

Prayer

Good God, your Spirit inspired the Sacred Scriptures that were read and fulfilled by your son in the synagogue. Give us a love of Scripture so that we might know you and your son more fully. Send us your spirit, enlivening our awareness of your work in our world. And thus may we be attentive to your voice, in word and world. **Amen.**

Today we read the beloved words of the apostle Paul, "Love is patient, love is kind." We pause to reflect on the times we have not embodied this love that "endures all things" . . .

Prayer

May we never sing a single note,
O God, without the sound of love
rising from our hearts, for love never fails with you.

Let our mouths declare God's justice *and our lives proclaim God's merciful love.* **Amen.**

Gospel   Luke 4:21-30

Jesus began speaking in the synagogue, saying: "Today this Scripture passage is fulfilled in your hearing." And all spoke highly of him and were amazed at the gracious words that came from his mouth. They also asked, "Isn't this the son of Joseph?" He said to them, "Surely you will quote me this proverb, 'Physician, cure yourself,' and say, 'Do here in your native place the things that we heard were done in Capernaum.'" And he said, "Amen, I say to you, no prophet is accepted in his own native place. Indeed, I tell you, there were many widows in Israel in the days of Elijah when the sky was closed for three and a half years and a severe famine spread over the entire land. It was to none of these that Elijah was sent, but only to a widow in Zarephath in the land of Sidon. Again, there were many lepers in Israel during the time of Elisha the prophet; yet not one of them was cleansed, but only Naaman the Syrian." When the people in the synagogue heard this, they were all filled with fury. They rose up, drove him out of the town, and led him to the brow of the hill on which their town had been built, to hurl him down headlong. But Jesus passed through the midst of them and went away.

Brief Silence

For Reflection

It can be difficult to be surprised by the familiar. Even people we encounter can become familiar to the point of predictability. So when someone familiar does something unexpected or different we can be puzzled. What follows might even be problematic. In these cases, it's usually best for us to reassess our expectations.

Something similar happens in today's gospel when Jesus preaches in his hometown synagogue. The audience thought they knew him: "Isn't this the son of Joseph?" In the face of such objection, Jesus does not change his message. On the contrary, he says that "no prophet is accepted in his own native place." By this, Jesus refers to himself as a prophet in the manner of Elisha and Elijah, prophets who went beyond the bounds of the Israelites, as Jesus will do. Jesus behaves in a way wholly unexpected by those in his hometown who ostensibly knew him best. Rather than seek to silence him for good, they might have reassessed their own preconceptions. But of course it's much easier to believe what I already "know" to be true. Today may we be open to the unexpected, for it might simply be the plan of God.

✦ In what ways can I be open to the unexpected?

Brief Silence

Prayer

God of surprises, give us an awareness to notice your presence when we are not expecting it. Open our eyes to your activity in our lives. May the unexpected and unplanned be moments of grace for us. We ask this in the name of your Son, Jesus our Lord, who himself knew how to be open to your will. **Amen.**

In today's gospel Jesus calls Peter, James, and John to be his first disciples. Peter responds by crying out, "Depart from me, Lord, for I am a sinful man." For the times we have let our own sinfulness prohibit us from following Jesus, we ask for mercy and forgiveness . . .

Prayer

Touch our lips, O God, and purify our hearts that we may respond to your call not only with words but with lives ready to follow you.

In the presence of the angels let us sing God's praise. *Let us give thanks to God's holy name.* **Amen.**

Gospel　　　　　　　　　　　　　　　　　　　**Luke 5:1-11**

While the crowd was pressing in on Jesus and listening to the word of God, he was standing by the Lake of Gennesaret. He saw two boats there alongside the lake; the fishermen had disembarked and were washing their nets. Getting into one of the boats, the one belonging to Simon, he asked him to put out a short distance from the shore. Then he sat down and taught the crowds from the boat. After he had finished speaking, he said to Simon, "Put out into deep water and lower your nets for a catch." Simon said in reply, "Master, we have worked hard all night and have caught nothing, but at your command I will lower the nets." When they had done this, they caught a great number of fish and their nets were tearing. They signaled to their partners in the other boat to come to help them. They came and filled both boats so that the boats were in danger of sinking. When Simon Peter saw this, he fell at the knees of Jesus and said, "Depart from me, Lord, for I am a sinful man." For astonishment at the catch of fish they had made seized him and all those with him, and likewise James and John, the sons of Zebedee, who were partners of Simon.

Jesus said to Simon, "Do not be afraid; from now on you will be catching men." When they brought their boats to the shore, they left everything and followed him.

Brief Silence

For Reflection

The call of Simon told by Luke is unique. Luke has a focus on Simon, without his brother Andrew. In fact, Luke mentions Andrew only in the list of the twelve (Luke 6:12; Acts 1:13) where he calls him the brother of Simon. Otherwise we hear nothing of Andrew from Luke. Luke also tells us in this story that Simon was "Simon Peter," prior to Jesus naming him "Peter." And we also hear about James and John, the sons of Zebedee, partners of Simon. According to Luke, this was not Simon's first encounter with Jesus, for earlier, Jesus healed Simon's mother-in-law (Luke 4:38-39). So after witnessing the power of Jesus in the healing of his mother-in-law and now in the miraculous catch of fish, Simon says, "Depart from me, Lord, for I am a sinful man." Jesus responds with a line that has reverberated through the centuries, "Do not be afraid; / from now on you will be catching men." What a difference this story is in the hands of the master storyteller Luke. We are in the hands of a remarkable theologian and evangelist. We would do well to read his story carefully and with attention to detail.

✦ In response to Peter's protestations of his own sinfulness, Jesus tells him, "Do not be afraid." Are there places in your own life where fear of failure keeps you from attempting something new? Can you hear Jesus telling you, "Do not be afraid"?

Brief Silence

Prayer

Spirit of truth and life, animate us with confidence and fortitude, knowing that we are chosen by God. Drive all fear from us so that we may be secure in our loving relationship with you. When anxiety grows, may your peace abound. Assured of our love in you, we pray. **Amen.**

Today, Jesus lays out for us the path to blessedness. For the times we have not followed this path by aligning ourselves with the poor and the hungry, we ask for pardon and forgiveness . . .

Prayer

Lord, keep our hearts turned always to you that we may be like trees planted by living water. May we be known by the good fruit we bear.

Blessed are they who hope in the Lord, *and walk by the light of God's law.* **Amen.**

Gospel   Luke 6:17, 20-26

Jesus came down with the Twelve and stood on a stretch of level ground with a great crowd of his disciples and a large number of the people from all Judea and Jerusalem and the coastal region of Tyre and Sidon. And raising his eyes toward his disciples he said: / "Blessed are you who are poor, / for the kingdom of God is yours. / Blessed are you who are now hungry, / for you will be satisfied. / Blessed are you who are now weeping, / for you will laugh. / Blessed are you when people hate you, and when they exclude and insult you, and denounce your name as evil on account of the Son of Man. Rejoice and leap for joy on that day! Behold, your reward will be great in heaven. For their ancestors treated the prophets in the same way. / But woe to you who are rich, / for you have received your consolation. / Woe to you who are filled now, / for you will be hungry. / Woe to you who laugh now, / for you will grieve and weep. / Woe to you when all speak well of you, / for their ancestors treated the false prophets in this way."

Brief Silence

For Reflection

Today in the Gospel of Luke we have Jesus' Sermon on the Plain as opposed to Matthew's Jesus who gives the Sermon on the Mount. Luke's Jesus preaches to a great crowd of disciples (indicating there were more than twelve) whereas Matthew's Jesus preaches to the disciples (and there were only twelve in the Gospel of Matthew).

But perhaps one of the greatest differences in the two versions of this story is not the setting or the audience but the message itself. Both Luke and Matthew begin with four beatitudes, but Matthew concludes with additional beatitudes. Luke, on the other hand, matches the four beatitudes with four woes that are frankly disturbing to the moderate middle-class listener from the developed world.

Luke has something to say to us today. This message is not limited to the time of Jesus. It is for us. Where do we find ourselves? In the four beatitudes or the four woes? This message is as much for us as it is for the disciples, if we dare to carry that name.

✦ In your daily life what are some actions you can take to align yourself with those Jesus proclaims as blessed: the poor, the hungry, the grieving, and the outcast?

Brief Silence

Prayer

Lord Jesus Christ, you blessed those considered unfortunate in the world. You reversed the ways and values of the powerful. Let your ways and values influence us deeply so that we will be known as your people in the world. May we be witnesses to you and therefore side with the marginalized in our day. **Amen.**

In today's gospel we hear the Golden Rule, "Do to others as you would have them do to you." We pause now to consider the times we have not lived up to this rule . . .

Prayer

There's a wideness in your mercy, Lord, large enough to fit even our greatest sins. Teach us the abundance of your compassion.

Bless the Lord, O my soul; *with all my breath, praise God's holy name.* **Amen.**

Gospel   Luke 6:27-38

Jesus said to his disciples: "To you who hear I say, love your enemies, do good to those who hate you, bless those who curse you, pray for those who mistreat you. To the person who strikes you on one cheek, offer the other one as well, and from the person who takes your cloak, do not withhold even your tunic. Give to everyone who asks of you, and from the one who takes what is yours do not demand it back. Do to others as you would have them do to you. For if you love those who love you, what credit is that to you? Even sinners love those who love them. And if you do good to those who do good to you, what credit is that to you? Even sinners do the same. If you lend money to those from whom you expect repayment, what credit is that to you? Even sinners lend to sinners, and get back the same amount. But rather, love your enemies and do good to them, and lend expecting nothing back; then your reward will be great and you will be children of the Most High, for he himself is kind to the ungrateful and the wicked. Be merciful, just as your Father is merciful.

"Stop judging and you will not be judged. Stop condemning and you will not be condemned. Forgive and you will be forgiven.

Give, and gifts will be given to you; a good measure, packed together, shaken down, and overflowing, will be poured into your lap. For the measure with which you measure will in return be measured out to you."

Brief Silence

For Reflection

Christians are to love their enemies, blessing them and praying for them. The Christian standard is one higher than what we could expect from the world with its transactional view of relationships. As Jesus himself notes, it's fairly easy to love those who love us, and to do good to those who do good to us. But it's another thing entirely to love those who are our enemies, to pray for them and to bless them.

We Christians are to be this way because God is this way. God is "kind to the ungrateful and the wicked." Should we be any different? We are to be merciful as the Father is merciful. And here we see in our own time the example of mercy given to us by Pope Francis. It is said that the word "mercy" is the hermeneutical key to his papacy. It is the way to understand and make sense of his actions. Pope Francis chose mercy because mercy is of God, and acting in this way demonstrates that we are followers of his son, Jesus.

✦ How does your family and/or parish follow Jesus' command to "bless those who curse you, pray for those who mistreat you"?

Brief Silence

Prayer

Lord Jesus, you call us to love our enemies and to pray for those who mistreat us. This standard can be difficult or seem out of reach. Grant us your spirit so that we may attain these lofty goals and be your witnesses. May our lives reflect your teachings and admonitions. We ask this in your holy name. **Amen.**

Jesus tells us today, "A good tree does not bear rotten fruit, / nor does a rotten tree bear good fruit. / For every tree is known by its own fruit." For the times we have failed to produce good fruit we ask for pardon and mercy . . .

Prayer

Strengthen our faith, Lord, that we may hold on to the word of life and bear the fruit of mercy in our hearts.

Proclaim God's kindness at dawn, *and sing praise to the Lord, Most High.* **Amen.**

Gospel   **Luke 6:39-45**

Jesus told his disciples a parable, "Can a blind person guide a blind person? Will not both fall into a pit? No disciple is superior to the teacher; but when fully trained, every disciple will be like his teacher. Why do you notice the splinter in your brother's eye, but do not perceive the wooden beam in your own? How can you say to your brother, 'Brother, let me remove that splinter in your eye,' when you do not even notice the wooden beam in your own eye? You hypocrite! Remove the wooden beam from your eye first; then you will see clearly to remove the splinter in your brother's eye.

"A good tree does not bear rotten fruit, nor does a rotten tree bear good fruit. For every tree is known by its own fruit. For people do not pick figs from thornbushes, nor do they gather grapes from brambles. A good person out of the store of goodness in his heart produces good, but an evil person out of a store of evil produces evil; for from the fullness of the heart the mouth speaks."

Brief Silence

For Reflection

The life lessons Jesus teaches in this gospel are akin to homespun wisdom rooted in daily life and experience. When we say a project at work is being performed like "the blind leading the blind" we are echoing Jesus' teaching. Though we mean no disrespect to the blind, the metaphor is easily grasped and understood.

And how often have we experienced the nitpicking nag who quickly points out the fault in others while conveniently overlooking his own. Jesus' warning about noticing the splinter in another's eye while neglecting the wooden beam in our own captures that sentiment well.

The concluding bit of wisdom is based on lived experience as well. "By their fruits you shall know them," is similar to, "actions speak louder than words." If a person is performing good works, it's likely they are a good person. On the other hand, if a person performs only selfish acts, that, too, is a window into their soul, for as Jesus puts it, "[F]rom the fullness of the heart the mouth speaks." A person's heart is ultimately known by their words and actions. And actions speak louder than words. These are words to live by.

✦ Sometimes we are most distressed by the faults of others that we also notice subconsciously in ourselves. Where have you become preoccupied with a "splinter in your brother's eye"? What might this preoccupation tell you about "the wooden beam in your own eye"?

Brief Silence

Prayer

Good teacher, Jesus, you give all good things including insights and advice for daily life. May we meditate on your words so that they dwell deeply in our hearts. Give us your attitudes and dispositions so that we might be more like you. We are your followers and seek to be known by your words and actions. We ask this in your name. **Amen.**

In a spirit of service we approach the Lenten season with prayer, fasting, and alms-giving, ever mindful of our destiny to be with Christ and his elect . . .

Prayer

In this acceptable time, on this day of salvation, teach us, Lord, to be merciful as we sing of your merciful love, and turn our hearts to you to follow your Gospel.

Blow the trumpet, and proclaim a fast, *for God is here with grace for his people.* **Amen.**

Gospel   Matt 6:1-6, 16-18

Jesus said to his disciples: "Take care not to perform righteous deeds in order that people may see them; otherwise, you will have no recompense from your heavenly Father. When you give alms, do not blow a trumpet before you, as the hypocrites do in the synagogues and in the streets to win the praise of others. Amen, I say to you, they have received their reward. But when you give alms, do not let your left hand know what your right is doing, so that your almsgiving may be secret. And your Father who sees in secret will repay you.

"When you pray, do not be like the hypocrites, who love to stand and pray in the synagogues and on street corners so that others may see them. Amen, I say to you, they have received their reward. But when you pray, go to your inner room, close the door, and pray to your Father in secret. And your Father who sees in secret will repay you.

"When you fast, do not look gloomy like the hypocrites. They neglect their appearance, so that they may appear to others to be fasting. Amen, I say to you, they have received their reward. But when you fast, anoint your head and wash your face, so that you may not appear to be fasting, except to your Father who is hidden. And your Father who sees what is hidden will repay you."

Brief Silence

For Reflection

Today, we'll likely see people with ashes on their foreheads indicating that they've been to Mass. It might seem strange that we do what the gospel exhorts us not to do! When we fast we are not to look gloomy but to wash our faces. We are also told to perform righteous deeds in secret; give alms, and pray in an inner room with no audience.

The exhortation from Jesus today is a reminder that crowds, neighbors, friends, or fellow Christians are not the audience for our works. Indeed, if they are, we have already received a reward. Instead, God the Father is our "audience" and it is He alone that we seek to impress, to put it in those terms.

There is a temptation among religious people to be seen or perceived as "doing it right." Many religious people take care to be seen at church. Perhaps they want others to know they've fulfilled their duty. That kind of attitude was prevalent in antiquity too. But that approach is not sufficient for a disciple of Christ. Our mission is to perform deeds of mercy for God the Father without seeking glory or attention from fellow human beings.

✦ How would you live this Lent if you knew it were your last?

Brief Silence

Prayer

Lord, Jesus Christ, you faced temptation and know from experience the human lives we lead. Be with us in these days of Lent so that we may know and feel your presence as we seek to follow you more closely. We ask this in your holy name. **Amen.**

In today's gospel Jesus is led out into the desert filled with the Holy Spirit. He remains there for forty days and is tempted by the devil. As we begin these forty days of fasting and prayer we ask for God's grace to sustain us and for the times we have given into temptation we ask for pardon and mercy . . .

Prayer

Free us, O God, from the temptation of not believing in our hearts what we sing with our mouths, for everyone who calls on your name will be saved.

Be with me, Lord, in time of trouble, *my God in whom I trust.* **Amen.**

Gospel   Luke 4:1-13

Filled with the Holy Spirit, Jesus returned from the Jordan and was led by the Spirit into the desert for forty days, to be tempted by the devil. He ate nothing during those days, and when they were over he was hungry. The devil said to him, "If you are the Son of God, command this stone to become bread." Jesus answered him, "It is written, *One does not live on bread alone.*" Then he took him up and showed him all the kingdoms of the world in a single instant. The devil said to him, "I shall give to you all this power and glory; for it has been handed over to me, and I may give it to whomever I wish. All this will be yours, if you worship me." Jesus said to him in reply, "It is written: / *You shall worship the Lord, your God, / and him alone shall you serve.*" / Then he led him to Jerusalem, made him stand on the parapet of the temple, and said to him, "If you are the Son of God, throw yourself down from here, for it is written: / *He will command his angels concerning you, to guard you, /* and: / *With their hands they will support you, / lest you dash your foot against a stone.*" / Jesus said to him in reply, "It also says, *You shall not put the Lord, your God, to the test.*" When the devil had finished every temptation, he departed from him for a time.

Brief Silence

For Reflection

Luke's version of the temptation of Jesus is more elaborate than the story we find in Mark. In fact, Mark tells the story (if we can even call it that) of the temptation in two verses whereas Luke uses thirteen (cf. Mark 1:12-13). Luke gives us a dialogue between Jesus and the devil that is completely absent in Mark. To each of the devil's temptations, some supported by Scripture, Jesus retorts with Scripture. The scene is almost one of a theological debating club.

Luke expanded on the story he inherited from Mark to convey theological insights and truths rather than compose a journalist's description of "what really happened." The church fathers knew that this story was meant to convey theology, and it was meant to be read metaphorically rather than literally.

As a master storyteller, Luke concludes the episode with three words that set the stage for later drama, namely, that the devil departed from him "for a time." We know that this was not to be the last encounter between the devil and Jesus. This first encounter with its triple temptations ultimately would lead to the Last Supper, the agony in the garden, the passion, and the cross.

✦ What helps you to remain steadfast in times of temptation?

Brief Silence

Prayer

Jesus Christ, son of God and son of Mary, grant to us we beseech you, the spirit of fortitude and courage that accompanied you in the wilderness. May that same spirit accompany us in times of trouble and temptation, so that we may be found to be faithful disciples. We ask this in your name, for you live and reign with the Father and the Spirit, one God forever and ever. **Amen.**

In today's gospel, Peter, John and James hear a voice from the cloud saying, "This is my chosen Son; listen to him." For the times we have not listened to the voice of Jesus, our Good Shepherd, we ask for pardon and mercy . . .

Prayer

Lord, it is good that we are here to sing your praise. But teach us to trust in your promise that we might follow you to the glory of the cross.

Stand firm in the Lord, the God of our ancestors. *Have courage, and wait for the Lord.* **Amen.**

Gospel   Luke 9:28b-36

Jesus took Peter, John, and James and went up the mountain to pray. While he was praying his face changed in appearance and his clothing became dazzling white. And behold, two men were conversing with him, Moses and Elijah, who appeared in glory and spoke of his exodus that he was going to accomplish in Jerusalem. Peter and his companions had been overcome by sleep, but becoming fully awake, they saw his glory and the two men standing with him. As they were about to part from him, Peter said to Jesus, "Master, it is good that we are here; let us make three tents, one for you, one for Moses, and one for Elijah." But he did not know what he was saying. While he was still speaking, a cloud came and cast a shadow over them, and they became frightened when they entered the cloud. Then from the cloud came a voice that said, "This is my chosen Son; listen to him." After the voice had spoken, Jesus was found alone. They fell silent and did not at that time tell anyone what they had seen.

Brief Silence

For Reflection

The presence of Elijah and Moses at the Transfiguration indicates Jesus as the fulfillment of the prophets (Elijah) and the law (Moses). Only three disciples are there to witness this terrific encounter, and they, too, are enveloped in the cloud, which itself is another image from the Old Testament.

More symbolism is present in the face of Jesus changing in appearance and his clothing becoming "dazzling white." There is so much that is symbolic and representative of Jesus' glory in this gospel reading that some scholars of Scripture refer to it as a "displaced resurrection account." In other words, this was originally a story of a resurrection appearance or a story about the risen Jesus that was transposed into the narrative of his earthly ministry by Mark (Matthew and Luke simply followed suit). Whether it is a displaced resurrection story or not, its Christology is profound, demonstrating that Jesus shares the glory of the Lord and fulfills the prophets and the law. He is on par with Elijah and Moses: He is called God's son, to whom we should listen.

✦ The voice from the cloud tells Peter, James, and John, "This is my chosen Son; listen to him." How do you listen to Jesus in daily life?

Brief Silence

Prayer

O God of the transcendent, you were present to the Israelites in their journey through the desert. You were present to Jesus at his baptism and transfiguration. Be present to us in our journeys. As we are made yours by baptism, make known to us our eternal destiny to be with you. We ask this through Christ our Lord, who was transfigured as your son. **Amen.**

In our first reading, God appears to Moses from a burning bush and gives him a mission to lead his people to freedom. As we prepare to enter into this liturgy, let us pause to consider how God might be calling to us this day, and to ask for mercy and pardon for the times we have not responded to this call . . .

Prayer

We stand on holy ground wherever we encounter your presence, O God. Help us be the face of Christ's mercy to the world.

Sing of God's blessing, O my soul, *our God whose mercy endures forever.* **Amen.**

Gospel   **Luke 13:1-9**

Some people told Jesus about the Galileans whose blood Pilate had mingled with the blood of their sacrifices. Jesus said to them in reply, "Do you think that because these Galileans suffered in this way they were greater sinners than all other Galileans? By no means! But I tell you, if you do not repent, you will all perish as they did! Or those eighteen people who were killed when the tower at Siloam fell on them—do you think they were more guilty than everyone else who lived in Jerusalem? By no means! But I tell you, if you do not repent, you will all perish as they did!"

And he told them this parable: "There once was a person who had a fig tree planted in his orchard, and when he came in search of fruit on it but found none, he said to the gardener, 'For three years now I have come in search of fruit on this fig tree but have found none. So cut it down. Why should it exhaust the soil?'

He said to him in reply, 'Sir, leave it for this year also, and I shall cultivate the ground around it and fertilize it; it may bear fruit in the future. If not you can cut it down.'"

Brief Silence

For Reflection

At the time of Jesus, when a tragic event happened at Siloam or when Pilate desecrated Jewish blood, the popular idea was that these people somehow had it coming. They must have done something bad for which they were punished. Jesus, however, interprets these events differently. He does not see this as a just punishment for some hidden sin. Instead, he tells those who are self-righteous in their smugness that the same will happen to them unless they repent. The period of time they have between witnessing the tragedy that befell others and the unknown time of their own death is a time for repentance. And the parable Jesus gives them underlines this point. The parable also subtly informs the audience that they have not been producing the fruit of good works. They have been given a limited amount of time to repent, but if that doesn't happen they, too, will be cut down like the barren fig tree, like those who suffered the tragedy at Siloam or desecration at the hands of Pilate. The message of today's gospel can be summarized in one simple word: Repent!

✦ Jesus gives us the parable of the barren fig tree. Where in your life, family, or parish is there a lack of fruit being borne? How might you cultivate the ground to encourage fruitfulness?

Brief Silence

Prayer

Good and gracious God, you call us to bear the good fruit of righteous deeds. Give us a spirit of service and self-sacrifice, so that we may put the needs of others before our own. May we be found worthy when our lives come to an end, having borne and produced good works, in imitation of your son, Our Lord, Jesus Christ. **Amen.**

In today's gospel we hear the familiar parable of the Prodigal Son. As we prepare to enter into this celebration, let us pause to consider the times we have wandered far from God and to ask for pardon and healing . . .

Prayer

Even before we speak a word, Father, you run to meet us and embrace us with love. Your banquet of mercy is prepared for all.

Let us savor the goodness of our gracious God, *whose song forever will fill our mouths.* **Amen.**

Gospel   **Luke 15:1-3, 11-32**

Tax collectors and sinners were all drawing near to listen to Jesus, but the Pharisees and scribes began to complain, saying, "This man welcomes sinners and eats with them." So to them Jesus addressed this parable: "A man had two sons, and the younger son said to his father, 'Father give me the share of your estate that should come to me.' So the father divided the property between them. After a few days, the younger son collected all his belongings and set off to a distant country where he squandered his inheritance on a life of dissipation. When he had freely spent everything, a severe famine struck that country, and he found himself in dire need. So he hired himself out to one of the local citizens who sent him to his farm to tend the swine. And he longed to eat his fill of the pods on which the swine fed, but nobody gave him any. Coming to his senses he thought, 'How many of my father's hired workers have more than enough food to eat, but here am I, dying from hunger. I shall get up and go to my father and I shall say to him, "Father, I have sinned against heaven and against you. I no longer deserve to be called your son; treat me as you would treat one of your hired workers."' So he got up and

went back to his father. While he was still a long way off, his
father caught sight of him, and was filled with compassion.
He ran to his son, embraced him and kissed him. His son said to
him, 'Father, I have sinned against heaven and against you; I no
longer deserve to be called your son.' But his father ordered his
servants, 'Quickly bring the finest robe and put it on him; put a
ring on his finger and sandals on his feet. Take the fattened calf
and slaughter it. Then let us celebrate with a feast, because this
son of mine was dead, and has come to life again; he was lost, and
has been found.' Then the celebration began. Now the older son
had been out in the field and, on his way back, as he neared the
house, he heard the sound of music and dancing. He called one of
the servants and asked what this might mean. The servant said to
him, 'Your brother has returned and your father has slaughtered
the fattened calf because he has him back safe and sound.' He
became angry, and when he refused to enter the house, his father
came out and pleaded with him. He said to his father in reply,
'Look, all these years I served you and not once did I disobey your
orders; yet you never gave me even a young goat to feast on with
my friends. But when your son returns who swallowed up your
property with prostitutes, for him you slaughter the fattened calf.'
He said to him, 'My son, you are here with me always; everything
I have is yours. But now we must celebrate and rejoice, because
your brother was dead and has come to life again; he was lost and
has been found.'"

Brief Silence

For Reflection
In today's telling, the story of the Prodigal Son is often interpreted
individually, as referring to a wayward person who has ultimately
been redeemed. The story is particularly meaningful to many
who have lived lives of regret or shame, only to feel the loving
embrace of God, a community of hope, a family, or even church
upon turning away from their wayward lifestyle.

But the story is sometimes interpreted so that the sons
represent Gentile (lost) and Jewish (favored) identities. In this,

the Gentiles have lost their way and lived generally wanton lives of decadence whereas Jews have followed the wishes of God. But in the end both sons, Gentile and Jew, receive the same reward.

One of the advantages of a parable is that it has so many possible interpretations. And this parable is told only by Luke. Without him we would know nothing of the Prodigal Son, and certainly nothing of the many works of art inspired by the parable, such as Rembrandt's "Return of the Prodigal Son." There is no sole or singular point to this story. The parable is polyvalent and ought to make us ponder it, as the church has done for centuries.

✦ Which figure in the parable of the Prodigal Son do you identify with the most at this point in your faith journey: the prodigal, the older son, or forgiving father? Why?

Brief Silence

Prayer

God Almighty, you forgive the penitent and welcome the sinner. Your mercy is boundless, and your generosity knows no limits. May we imitate your spirit of compassion and kindness, reaching beyond ourselves to practice forgiveness and empathy. In doing so may we extend the love of your Son, Jesus Christ, into the world. We ask this in his name. **Amen.**

In today's gospel Jesus tells the accusers of the adulterous woman, "Let the one among you who is without sin / be the first to throw a stone at her." For the times we have cast stones of accusation and condemnation at our brothers and sisters let us ask for God's mercy and forgiveness . . .

Prayer

Our sins are laid bare before you, O God. Still you do not remember the cause of our shame, but you open a way and make all things new.

Return to the Lord with rejoicing. *Let our hearts sing of God's great mercy.* **Amen.**

Gospel   John 8:1-11

Jesus went to the Mount of Olives. But early in the morning he arrived again in the temple area, and all the people started coming to him, and he sat down and taught them. Then the scribes and the Pharisees brought a woman who had been caught in adultery and made her stand in the middle. They said to him, "Teacher, this woman was caught in the very act of committing adultery. Now in the law, Moses commanded us to stone such women. So what do you say?" They said this to test him, so that they could have some charge to bring against him. Jesus bent down and began to write on the ground with his finger. But when they continued asking him, he straightened up and said to them, "Let the one among you who is without sin be the first to throw a stone at her." Again he bent down and wrote on the ground. And in response, they went away one by one, beginning with the elders. So he was left alone with the woman before him.

Then Jesus straightened up and said to her, "Woman, where are they? Has no one condemned you?" She replied, "No one, sir." Then Jesus said, "Neither do I condemn you. Go, and from now on do not sin any more."

Brief Silence

For Reflection

There was a time in church history, a few centuries after Jesus' death and resurrection, that some Christians did not believe in forgiveness of sin after one's baptism. As a result, many Christians were delaying baptism until well after their "sinning years" were over, effectively delaying baptism until one's deathbed! But that can be a difficult time to predict. Other Christians were proclaiming what was perceived to be a more libertine attitude, namely, that one could be forgiven for sins even after one was baptized.

In the face of such internal church disputes comes this story about Jesus. That is to say, it was about the time that the church was engaging in the debate about forgiveness of sins that the story of Jesus forgiving the woman caught in adultery began to appear in early manuscripts. It's as though the church recalled an episode from Jesus' life, or told a story about how Jesus might approach the issue. The story in today's gospel is a prominent post in the journey of how the church went from Jesus' personal ministry to the sacrament of reconciliation we have today.

✦ Jesus gives us a model of mercy in today's gospel. How have you experienced giving and receiving mercy in your own life of faith?

Brief Silence

Prayer

Spirit of compassion and mercy, be with us in times of decision and judgment. May we look with the eyes of Jesus, practicing forgiveness at each opportunity, slow to anger and rich in kindness. May our expression of patient, loving kindness reflect the love that God has for each of us. We ask this in the name of Jesus, the incarnation of love, compassion, and mercy. **Amen.**

On this feast of Palm Sunday we read from St. Paul's letter to the Philippians the ancient hymn of Jesus' glory. The Son of God emptied himself and became obedient unto death, death on a cross. Let us pause now to empty ourselves so there might be room within us for the Lord of Life to dwell . . .

Prayer

Pierce our hearts, O God, with love for your Son, Jesus. As we enter the Mystery of his dying and rising, may our voices and lives give you worthy praise.

With all your people, I will praise you, Lord. *I will glorify your name forever.* **Amen.**

Gospel   **Luke 22:14–23:56 (or Luke 23:1-49)**

The elders of the people, chief priests and scribes, arose and brought Jesus before Pilate. They brought charges against him, saying, "We found this man misleading our people; he opposes the payment of taxes to Caesar and maintains that he is the Christ, a king." Pilate asked him, "Are you the king of the Jews?" He said to him in reply, "You say so." Pilate then addressed the chief priests and the crowds, "I find this man not guilty." But they were adamant and said, "He is inciting the people with his teaching throughout all Judea, from Galilee where he began even to here."

On hearing this Pilate asked if the man was a Galilean; and upon learning that he was under Herod's jurisdiction, he sent him to Herod who was in Jerusalem at that time. Herod was very glad to see Jesus; he had been wanting to see him for a long time, for he had heard about him and had been hoping to see him perform some sign. He questioned him at length, but he gave him no answer. The chief priests and scribes, meanwhile, stood by accusing him harshly. Herod and his soldiers treated him contemptuously and mocked him, and after clothing him in resplendent garb, he sent him back to Pilate. Herod and Pilate became friends that very day, even though they had been enemies formerly. Pilate then summoned the chief priests, the rulers, and the people and said to them, "You brought this man to me and accused him of inciting the people to revolt. I have conducted my investigation in your presence and have not found this man guilty of the charges you have brought against him, nor did Herod, for he sent him back to us. So no capital crime has been committed by him. Therefore I shall have him flogged and then release him."

But all together they shouted out, "Away with this man! Release Barabbas to us."—Now Barabbas had been imprisoned for a rebellion that had taken place in the city and for murder.—Again Pilate addressed them, still wishing to release Jesus, but they continued their shouting, "Crucify him! Crucify him!" Pilate addressed them a third time, "What evil has this man done? I found him guilty of no capital crime. Therefore I shall have him flogged and then release him." With loud shouts, however, they persisted in calling for his crucifixion, and their voices prevailed. The verdict of Pilate was that their demand should be granted. So he released the man who had been imprisoned for rebellion and murder, for whom they asked, and he handed Jesus over to them to deal with as they wished.

As they led him away they took hold of a certain Simon, a Cyrenian, who was coming in from the country; and after laying the cross on him, they made him carry it behind Jesus. A large crowd of people followed Jesus, including many women who mourned and lamented him. Jesus turned to them and said, "Daughters of Jerusalem, do not weep for me; weep instead for yourselves and for your children for indeed, the days are coming when people will say, 'Blessed are the barren, the wombs that never bore and the breasts that never nursed.' At that time people will say to the mountains, 'Fall upon us!' and to the hills, 'Cover us!' for if these things are done when the wood is green what will happen when it is dry?" Now two others, both criminals, were led away with him to be executed.

When they came to the place called the Skull, they crucified him and the criminals there, one on his right, the other on his left. Then Jesus said, "Father, forgive them, they know not what they do." They divided his garments by casting lots. The people stood by and watched; the rulers, meanwhile, sneered at him and said, "He saved others, let him save himself if he is the chosen one, the Christ of God." Even the soldiers jeered at him. As they approached to offer him wine they called out, "If you are King of the Jews, save yourself." Above him there was an inscription that read, "This is the King of the Jews."

Now one of the criminals hanging there reviled Jesus, saying, "Are you not the Christ? Save yourself and us." The other, however, rebuking him, said in reply, "Have you no fear of God, for you are subject to the same condemnation? And indeed, we have been condemned justly, for the sentence we received corresponds to our crimes, but this man has done nothing criminal." Then he said, "Jesus, remember me when you come into your kingdom." He replied to him, "Amen, I say to you, today you will be with me in Paradise."

It was now about noon and darkness came over the whole land until three in the afternoon because of an eclipse of the sun. Then the veil of the temple was torn down the middle. Jesus cried out in a loud voice, "Father, into your hands I commend my spirit"; and when he had said this he breathed his last.

Here all kneel and pause for a short time.

The centurion who witnessed what had happened glorified God and said, "This man was innocent beyond doubt." When all the people who had gathered for this spectacle saw what had happened, they returned home beating their breasts; but all his acquaintances stood at a distance, including the women who had followed him from Galilee and saw these events.

Brief Silence

For Reflection

We are fickle creatures. We can experience happiness to the point of being ecstatic one minute and sink to the depths of despair the next. The church attempts to capture and express this fickleness in the liturgy today when we enter with palm branches singing songs of praise, only to cry out in unison moments later during the gospel, "Crucify him! Crucify him!"

The power of Christ is on display in this gospel when Jesus prays from the cross, "Father, forgive them." And the mercy of Jesus extends even to a criminal, which Luke relates to us in an exchange between them. The profundity of this forgiveness is something that we reflect upon year after year. We will not exhaust this story. It will exhaust us, and we shall return to it to gain insight, understanding, and strength.

Let's soak up the gospel today and try to keep our fickleness in check. Let's wave palm branches and sing songs of praise without losing ourselves in a call to "Crucify him! Crucify him!" But even if, and perhaps when, we do, we know that forgiveness awaits from a merciful God.

✦ How have you experienced God's forgiveness in your own life?

Brief Silence

Prayer

God, the Father of mercies, you sent your Son into the world because you love the world. Our response to your love has not been equal to the generosity of your gift. Give us the wisdom to choose love over hate, patient thought over quick judgment, and forgiveness over condemnation. **Amen.**

In the washing of his disciples' feet, Jesus has given us a model of humility and service. As he has done, so we are to do. Let us pause to ask forgiveness for the times we have failed to serve God and one another . . .

Prayer

Though Master, you bend down to wash your disciples' feet, and you call us to imitate your example. May these Three Days of memorial teach us to love like you.

Let us offer our sacrifice of praise *and sing of the Lord's goodness.* **Amen.**

Gospel   **John 13:1-15**

Before the feast of Passover, Jesus knew that his hour had come to pass from this world to the Father. He loved his own in the world and he loved them to the end. The devil had already induced Judas, son of Simon the Iscariot, to hand him over. So, during supper, fully aware that the Father had put everything into his power and that he had come from God and was returning to God, he rose from supper and took off his outer garments. He took a towel and tied it around his waist. Then he poured water into a basin and began to wash the disciples' feet and dry them with the towel around his waist. He came to Simon Peter, who said to him, "Master, are you going to wash my feet?" Jesus answered and said to him, "What I am doing, you do not understand now, but you will understand later." Peter said to him, "You will never wash my feet." Jesus answered him, "Unless I wash you, you will have no inheritance with me." Simon Peter said to him, "Master, then not only my feet, but my hands and head as well." Jesus said to him, "Whoever has bathed has no need except to have his feet washed, for he is clean all over; so you are clean, but not all." For he knew who would betray him; for this reason, he said, "Not all of you are clean."

So when he had washed their feet and put his garments back on and reclined at table again, he said to them, "Do you realize what I have done for you? You call me 'teacher' and 'master,' and rightly so, for indeed I am. If I, therefore, the master and teacher, have washed your feet, you ought to wash one another's feet. I have given you a model to follow, so that as I have done for you, you should also do."

Brief Silence

For Reflection

This evening as we celebrate the institution of the Eucharist, we listen to the sole gospel that does not include that story! John situates the Last Supper on the night before Passover, as the opening verses of this evening's gospel reading indicate. No Passover meal is needed at the Last Supper, especially when we consider that for this gospel, Jesus is understood to be the Lamb of God. And we shall see that the crucifixion takes place on the day of preparation, when the lambs are being slaughtered in *preparation* for Passover later that night.

So the Last Supper for the Gospel of John is not about Eucharist as much as service. Jesus the master becomes the servant of his disciples, thus giving them an example. By so doing, Jesus exemplifies a core message of the gospel, and core message of his own identity. If we are to follow Jesus, we, too, must become servants. There will never be a time when we are content to sit back, relax, and be served. Instead, we are the ones who serve, in imitation of Jesus, our master, and the one true servant of God.

✦ In today's gospel Jesus tells Peter, "Unless I wash you, you will have no inheritance with me." How has serving or being served affected your understanding of being a Christian?

Brief Silence

Prayer

Jesus Christ, Servant-Master, you gave us an example to follow. May we be servants of others in imitation of you. May our lives be lived for others rather than for ourselves alone. Give us a spirit of generosity and self-gift so that we may be known as your disciples. We ask this in your holy name. **Amen.**

Christ is risen, alleluia! We gather together on this feast of life that is stronger than death and ask the Lord to bring light to the darkness within us . . .

Prayer

Christians, to the Paschal Lamb: *Sing your thankful praises to God!*

The Prince of Life has conquered death: *Sing your thankful praises to God!*

The empty tomb is filled with blessing: *Sing your thankful praises to God!*

For Christ is risen! Alleluia! Alleluia! *Christ is risen indeed! Alleluia! Alleluia!* **Amen.**

Gospel
John 20:1-9

On the first day of the week, Mary of Magdala came to the tomb early in the morning, while it was still dark, and saw the stone removed from the tomb. So she ran and went to Simon Peter and to the other disciple whom Jesus loved, and told them, "They have taken the Lord from the tomb, and we don't know where they put him." So Peter and the other disciple went out and came to the tomb. They both ran, but the other disciple ran faster than Peter and arrived at the tomb first; he bent down and saw the burial cloths there, but did not go in. When Simon Peter arrived after him, he went into the tomb and saw the burial cloths there, and the cloth that had covered his head, not with the burial cloths but rolled up in a separate place. Then the other disciple also went in, the one who had arrived at the tomb first, and he saw and believed. For they did not yet understand the Scripture that he had to rise from the dead.

Brief Silence

For Reflection

In John's account of the empty tomb Mary seems to be alone, and upon finding the stone turned away, she runs to Simon Peter and the disciple whom Jesus loved. We need to read further in the gospel than what we hear in today's liturgy to find out more about Mary's role on that morning. The gospel reading for today is content to have Mary fetch Peter and the other disciple. We hear no more about her. This other disciple, the one whom Jesus loved, is the first to believe, even though neither he nor Peter at that time understood the Scripture about rising from the dead.

So this becomes something of a model of faith. We, like the beloved disciple, believe before we understand completely. Upon believing, we spend the rest of our lives contemplating the mystery of faith. And like the Beloved Disciple we are led to faith by another, in this case Mary of Magdala. She is the one who indicates that the stone was rolled away. She points to something that needs to be explored, investigated. And once the Beloved Disciple has that encounter the response is faith.

✦ At the empty tomb the Beloved Disciple believes but does not yet understand. What mysteries of faith do you lack understanding of? How might God be calling you to strengthen your belief?

Brief Silence

Prayer

Jesus Christ, risen from the dead, you give us hope of life eternal. When days seem dark and night long, may your Easter spirit animate us with the promise of a new day filled with light and life. With the knowledge that your resurrection conquered death itself, we are confident in our request. **Amen.**

In the waters of baptism we have been buried with Christ, the one who tells St. John in Revelation, "I am the first and the last, the one who lives." May this water remind us of the life that conquers death . . .

Prayer

Give thanks to the Lord, for God is good: *God's love is everlasting!*
Let all that has breath sing praise to God: *God's love is everlasting!*
God casts all fear and doubt away: *God's love is everlasting!*
Christ is risen! Alleluia! Alleluia! *Christ is risen indeed! Alleluia!*
Alleluia! **Amen.**

Gospel   **John 20:19-31**

On the evening of that first day of the week, when the doors were locked, where the disciples were, for fear of the Jews, Jesus came and stood in their midst and said to them, "Peace be with you." When he had said this, he showed them his hands and his side. The disciples rejoiced when they saw the Lord. Jesus said to them again, "Peace be with you. As the Father has sent me, so I send you." And when he had said this, he breathed on them and said to them, "Receive the Holy Spirit. Whose sins you forgive are forgiven them, and whose sins you retain are retained."

Thomas, called Didymus, one of the Twelve, was not with them when Jesus came. So the other disciples said to him, "We have seen the Lord." But he said to them, "Unless I see the mark of the nails in his hands and put my finger into the nailmarks and put my hand into his side, I will not believe."

Now a week later his disciples were again inside and Thomas was with them. Jesus came, although the doors were locked, and stood in their midst and said, "Peace be with you." Then he said to Thomas, "Put your finger here and see my hands, and bring your hand and put it into my side, and do not be unbelieving, but believe." Thomas answered and said to him, "My Lord and my God!" Jesus said to him, "Have you come to believe because you have seen me? Blessed are those who have not seen and have believed."

Now Jesus did many other signs in the presence of his disciples that are not written in this book. But these are written that you may come to believe that Jesus is the Christ, the Son of God, and that through this belief you may have life in his name.

Brief Silence

For Reflection

In today's gospel reading Thomas encounters the risen Christ the week after the initial resurrection appearance. He has been called "doubting Thomas," even though the word "doubt" does not appear in the story. Still, it's clear Thomas was hesitant to believe. More than one preacher has likened Thomas' attitude to a "show me" skepticism. His belief is conditioned on physically inspecting the risen Christ. And yet, the story does not say that when given the opportunity Thomas actually probed the nail marks or put his hand in Jesus' side. Instead, upon encountering the risen Christ he immediately proclaims, "My Lord and my God!" What the reader has known from the opening verses of the gospel—"In the beginning was the Word, / and the Word was with God, / and the Word was God. . . . And the Word became flesh" (John 1:1, 14; NABRE)—is effectively proclaimed by a human being, Thomas. Then Jesus appropriately has the last word, and the gospel concludes with two verses from the author. The Gospel of John has a profound Christology. The closing verses of chapter 20 give us some indication as to why.

✦ Jesus tells the disciples, "Peace be with you," three times in today's gospel. Where in your life are you in need of the peace of the Lord?

Brief Silence

Prayer

Lord God, giver of peace, you grant gifts the world cannot give.
May your peace settle over us completely, driving away all
anxiety. Confident in the knowledge that we are yours, we thank
you for your munificence. **Amen.**

In today's gospel, Simon Peter recognizes the risen Lord on the shores of the Sea of Galilee and immediately jumps from his boat into the water. May this sprinkling rite symbolize our own desire to be close to Jesus . . .

Prayer

You show mercy on all your people, O God, through the boundless love of your Son, Jesus. Truly worthy is the Lamb that was slain for us.

Sing praise to the Lord, you faithful ones. Alleluia! *And give thanks to God's holy name. Alleluia!* **Amen.**

Gospel
John 21:1-14 (or John 21:1-19)

At that time, Jesus revealed himself again to his disciples at the Sea of Tiberias. He revealed himself in this way. Together were Simon Peter, Thomas called Didymus, Nathanael from Cana in Galilee, Zebedee's sons, and two others of his disciples. Simon Peter said to them, "I am going fishing." They said to him, "We also will come with you." So they went out and got into the boat, but that night they caught nothing. When it was already dawn, Jesus was standing on the shore; but the disciples did not realize that it was Jesus. Jesus said to them, "Children, have you caught anything to eat?" They answered him, "No." So he said to them, "Cast the net over the right side of the boat and you will find something." So they cast it, and were not able to pull it in because of the number of fish. So the disciple whom Jesus loved said to Peter, "It is the Lord." When Simon Peter heard that it was the Lord, he tucked in his garment, for he was lightly clad, and jumped into the sea. The other disciples came in the boat, for they were not far from shore, only about a hundred yards, dragging the net with the fish. When they climbed out on shore, they saw a charcoal fire with fish on it and bread. Jesus said to them, "Bring some of the fish you just caught." So Simon Peter went over and dragged the net ashore full of one hundred fifty-three large fish. Even though there were so many, the net was not torn. Jesus said to them, "Come, have breakfast." And none of the disciples dared to ask him, "Who are you?" because they realized it was the Lord. Jesus came over and took the bread and gave it to them, and in like manner the fish. This was now the third time Jesus was revealed to his disciples after being raised from the dead.

Brief Silence

For Reflection

Today's reading incorporates two stories: one of the appearance on the seashore, followed by another of the rehabilitation of Peter. The Beloved Disciple, who remains nameless, is the first to recognize Jesus with the proclamation, "It is the Lord" (John 21:7). This is an echo of the discovery of the empty tomb when, even though Peter was the first to go into the empty tomb, the Beloved Disciple "saw and believed" (John 20:8; NABRE).

Another nod to earlier stories in the Gospel of John include the mention of a "charcoal fire," as that is the place where Peter denied Jesus three times (John 18:18; NABRE). The presence of a charcoal fire here sets the stage, narratively speaking, for his threefold rehabilitation. Three times Jesus asks Peter, "Do you love me?" and three times Peter responds affirmatively. Though he denied Jesus, Peter was effectively forgiven and placed in a leadership role. Thus in the Christian imagination, Peter represents the ideals and realities of discipleship. No Christian community is an island unto itself. Even leaders can stumble; when they do they can be forgiven by Jesus himself. Such is the power of the risen Christ.

✦ Who are the lambs that Jesus has given you to tend and feed? How do you serve them?

Brief Silence

Prayer

Lord, Jesus, Lamb of God, you take away the sins of the world. You rose from the dead and gave us the command above all others, to love one another. May our lives be filled with love for you, our fellow human beings, and all those we encounter. Unencumbered by sin, may we experience the fullness of your risen life. We ask this in your name. **Amen.**

In the waters of baptism we entered the church, the sheepfold of the Lord. May this water remind us of the joy of that day and strengthen us in our baptismal promises . . .

Prayer

Under your care, Good Shepherd, we find shelter and peace, and no longer do we hunger or thirst. Teach us to hear and follow your voice.

Sing joyfully to the Lord, all you lands. Alleluia! *Come before our God with joyful song. Alleluia!*

Amen.

Gospel   John 10:27-30

Jesus said: "My sheep hear my voice; I know them, and they follow me. I give them eternal life, and they shall never perish. No one can take them out of my hand. My Father, who has given them to me, is greater than all, and no one can take them out of the Father's hand. The Father and I are one."

Brief Silence

For Reflection

Though we are in Cycle C (the Gospel of Luke), today we have another reading from the Gospel of John. Each week since Easter we have read from John. Today we read about the familiar, comforting image of Jesus as the good shepherd. We are his sheep who hear his voice and respond by following him.

The symbolism is profound and perhaps even more so because the snippet we read today is so short. The meaning of the words should not be lost in their brevity. The relationship of the sheep to the shepherd is dependent upon the Father and Jesus. The Father has given the sheep to Jesus. No one can take them from the Father or the Son, for the Father and the Son are one.

Given the symbolism, the task of the sheep is pure and simple, to follow Jesus, to be a disciple. The task of the Father and the Son is not to lose the sheep, or perhaps not to give them up to those who might try to pry open their hands. Our task, therefore, is no more difficult than following Jesus. To do that we must be attentive to his voice.

✦ How do you listen for the voice of the Good Shepherd in your daily life?

Brief Silence

Prayer

Jesus, you are the Good Shepherd who calls us, your sheep. We strive to respond to your voice and to follow you. When the noise of the world makes it difficult to hear you, give us ears attentive to your call. For then we shall know the way to go, home to you. May we be yours from now until eternity. **Amen.**

In the waters of baptism we are washed clean of sin and filled with the grace and love of God. May this water renew our hearts and spirits to be signs of God's love and life on the earth . . .

Prayer

Gracious God, you make all things new in your love. Help us be known by our love for one another that we may be your true disciples.

Let all your creatures give you thanks, O God. Alleluia! *May all your children bless you. Alleluia!* **Amen.**

Gospel   John 13:31-33a, 34-35

When Judas had left them, Jesus said, "Now is the Son of Man glorified, and God is glorified in him. If God is glorified in him, God will also glorify him in himself, and God will glorify him at once. My children, I will be with you only a little while longer. I give you a new commandment: love one another. As I have loved you, so you also should love one another. This is how all will know that you are my disciples, if you have love for one another."

Brief Silence

For Reflection

We continue reading from the Gospel of John during the Easter season. This evangelist has unique things to say about Jesus, and he relates stories about Jesus not found anywhere else. Our gospel reading for today is a case in point. Other gospels have Jesus saying, "Love your neighbor," (Matt 19:19; Mark 12:31; Luke 10:27; NABRE) or even, "Love your enemies" (Matt 5:44; Luke 6:27; NABRE). But today we hear the simple but profound command to "love one another," which presumes that there are others in the community. In cases where semantics can open a debate about "who is my neighbor?" or how precisely we "love" an "enemy," the command to love one another is straightforward and leaves little room for negotiation or explanation. Further, it is a command related to "one another," which means those in the Christian community closest to us. In some senses it harkens to family, and the relationships we have with one another as family. It's nearly a plea for siblings to do more than "get along" but to actually "love one another." For the Fourth Gospel, all ethical commands of Jesus may be summed up in this one command to love.

✦ Jesus gives us a new commandment: "[L]ove one another." How do you show love for the people closest to you?

Brief Silence

Prayer

Good and gracious God, you sent your son into the world because you so loved the world. Your son gave us the commandment to love. Give us a spirit of gracious love so that we may pour ourselves out in service to all those we meet. In so doing we will be imitating Jesus, your son, the incarnation of love. We ask this in his name, for he lives and reigns with you and the Spirit, one God forever and ever. **Amen.**

Through the waters of Baptism we are given new life in the Spirit of God. May this sprinkling rite renew us in joy, hope, and love . . .

Prayer

Peace is your gift to your people, O God, the peace the world cannot give. Let the light of your peace shine brightly over all the earth.

All you nations, praise the Lord. Alleluia! *Be glad and exult, all people of God. Alleluia!* **Amen.**

Gospel   John 14:23-29

Jesus said to his disciples: "Whoever loves me will keep my word, and my Father will love him, and we will come to him and make our dwelling with him. Whoever does not love me does not keep my words; yet the word you hear is not mine but that of the Father who sent me.

"I have told you this while I am with you. The Advocate, the Holy Spirit, whom the Father will send in my name, will teach you everything and remind you of all that I told you. Peace I leave with you; my peace I give to you. Not as the world gives do I give it to you. Do not let your hearts be troubled or afraid. You heard me tell you, 'I am going away and I will come back to you.' If you loved me, you would rejoice that I am going to the Father; for the Father is greater than I. And now I have told you this before it happens, so that when it happens you may believe."

Brief Silence

For Reflection

A gift of Jesus given to the disciples is peace, but Jesus is quick to say that it's not the peace given by the world, but that given by Jesus. The world's peace can be understood as the absence of war, or a cessation of hostilities. Others interpret it as the peace gained by domination of subject peoples. And in Jesus' time the Romans were the occupying power. A generation after Jesus the city of Jerusalem with its temple would be destroyed by Rome. At the conclusion of that campaign the Romans would say they pacified Judea! The death, destruction, slaughter, fire, and pillaging of Jerusalem and its temple meant for the Romans that the land was at peace! So, no, Jesus' peace is not like that given by the world, given by the Romans.

Jesus gives an interior wholeness, to be at peace with oneself and the world around us. The inner disposition of a disciple is one of peace, not aggression, peace, rather than anger, peace not hostility, peace rather than anxiety, peace not pursuit of ill-gotten gain. The life of a disciple is marked by the gift of peace given by Jesus.

✦ How do you experience the peace of Christ in your daily life?

Brief Silence

Prayer

Risen Lord, bringer and giver of peace, your gift is not like that given by the world. Your peace satisfies the deepest human longings, the deepest human desires. Give that same peace to us now, so that secure in ourselves we may live for you. With an interior wholeness that only you grant, we face the challenges of each day. In your name we pray. **Amen.**

Jesus tells us today, "[Y]ou will be my witnesses in Jerusalem, / throughout Judea and Samaria, / and to the ends of the earth." May this water sprinkled over us strengthen our resolve to witness to the love of Jesus in all aspects of our lives . . .

Prayer

You have made us witnesses to all the earth, O God, to announce the message: Do not fear, for Christ is risen! For this may we never cease to praise you.

Sing praise to God, sing praise. Alleluia! *All people of God, sing hymns of praise. Alleluia!* **Amen.**

Gospel   Luke 24:46-53

Jesus said to his disciples: "Thus it is written that the Christ would suffer and rise from the dead on the third day and that repentance, for the forgiveness of sins, would be preached in his name to all the nations, beginning from Jerusalem. You are witnesses of these things. And behold I am sending the promise of my Father upon you; but stay in the city until you are clothed with power from on high."

Then he led them out as far as Bethany, raised his hands, and blessed them. As he blessed them he parted from them and was taken up to heaven. They did him homage and then returned to Jerusalem with great joy, and they were continually in the temple praising God.

Brief Silence

For Reflection

Importantly, we are reading today from the Gospel of Luke, where the ascension of Jesus takes place near Jerusalem on Easter Sunday evening. Later, when Luke writes the Acts of the Apostles, he says that the ascension took place forty days after Easter (Acts 1:9-11). Luke is keen to indicate both in the gospel and in Acts that there was a time when the resurrection appearances to the disciples came to an end. After that time Jesus would be known in the "breaking of the bread" (Luke 24:35; NABRE).

So, according the Gospel of Luke, the story has come full circle. What began in the Jerusalem temple with the appearance to Zechariah (Luke 1:9) has now been completed with the ascension from Jerusalem. The disciples are left praising God in the temple for the wondrous works he has done in and through Jesus. No longer will they witness the risen Christ, but from now on, they know him in the breaking of the bread. We too, come to know Jesus as the disciples did, in the breaking of the bread.

✦ The Gospel of Luke ends where it began, in Jerusalem. Often our lives seem cyclical. Where and when did your spiritual journey begin? Where is the journey taking you now?

Brief Silence

Prayer

Spirit of God, you raised Jesus to heaven where he lives and reigns forever. Continue to make us mindful of our eternal destiny to be with him. With this knowledge ever before us, we continue on the journey, eyes on our heavenly home. In the name of this same Jesus we pray. **Amen.**

In baptism we are born into the universal church, the Body of Christ. May the sprinkling of this water strengthen us in unity with one another and with Christians throughout the world . . .

Prayer

Make us one, O God, by your Spirit of love, and remove whatever divides us. In Christ may we be united in peace.

The Lord is Most High over all the earth. Alleluia! *God rules all people with mercy. Alleluia!* **Amen.**

Gospel **John 17:20-26**

Lifting up his eyes to heaven, Jesus prayed, saying: "Holy Father, I pray not only for them, but also for those who will believe in me through their word, so that they may all be one, as you, Father, are in me and I in you, that they also may be in us, that the world may believe that you sent me. And I have given them the glory you gave me, so that they may be one, as we are one, I in them and you in me, that they may be brought to perfection as one, that the world may know that you sent me, and that you loved them even as you loved me. Father, they are your gift to me. I wish that where I am they also may be with me, that they may see my glory that you gave me, because you loved me before the foundation of the world. Righteous Father, the world also does not know you, but I know you, and they know that you sent me. I made known to them your name and I will make it known, that the love with which you loved me may be in them and I in them."

Brief Silence

For Reflection

In the Gospel we hear Jesus' prayer for his followers, not only his living breathing disciples at the time, but all those who will "believe in me through their word." That is, he is praying for us today. And he is praying for us that we all might be one. Unfortunately, we only need to look out on the street corners of our towns, villages, and cities to see that we are not one in Christ. There are many, many denominations split by creedal statements, doctrinal beliefs, ethical practices, treatment and role of women, sexual orientation, care for the earth, and more. Sadly, Jesus' prayer has not yet been realized. And we know from the Johannine literature (Gospel of John, 1 John, 2 John, and 3 John) that the early community faced ruptures and schisms too. So that reality is not new to us, or new to the Reformation in the sixteenth century. As long as there have been Christians there has unfortunately been disunity.

So if we Christians want the world to believe, we might start with reconciling ourselves to one another. According to the words of Jesus in this gospel, Christian unity will cause the world to know Christ.

✦ Jesus prays for unity among his followers. Where do you see division in your local Christian community? How might you work for unity?

Brief Silence

Prayer

Lord God, source of all unity, unite us in love for your son and for one another. May we see past external differences to focus on internal truths and essentials. Bound together into one body, we recognize that what happens to one affects all. Give us concern for all so that we may rise together. In Christ your son. **Amen.**

On the Third Sunday of Advent we heard John the Baptist proclaim that the one who was to come would baptize with the Holy Spirit and with fire. And now on the Feast of Pentecost we see this come true. In baptism we are baptized into the life of the Holy Spirit. May this water rekindle the fire of the Holy Spirit within us . . .

Prayer

From your celestial home: *Come, Holy Spirit, come!*
The Source of all that is good: *Come, Holy Spirit, come!*
Most blessed Light divine: *Come, Holy Spirit, come!*
Fill the hearts of your faithful. Alleluia! *And kindle in them the fire of your love. Alleluia!*
 Amen.

Gospel   **John 14:15-16, 23b-26 (or John 20:19-23)**

Jesus said to his disciples: "If you love me, you will keep my commandments. And I will ask the Father, and he will give you another Advocate to be with you always.

"Whoever loves me will keep my word, and my Father will love him, and we will come to him and make our dwelling with him. Those who do not love me do not keep my words; yet the word you hear is not mine but that of the Father who sent me.

"I have told you this while I am with you. The Advocate, the Holy Spirit whom the Father will send in my name, will teach you everything and remind you of all that I told you."

Brief Silence

For Reflection

We are now about fifty days, or seven weeks, from Easter. To be clear, Pentecost was a Jewish feast of the springtime. Because it comes about fifty days (Lev 23:16) after the feast of Passover it was also called Pentecost (which means "fifty" in Greek).

But the Gospel of John seems not to know anything about the feast of Pentecost and the emboldened Peter preaching, as we have it in Acts. Instead, the story we have in John takes place on Easter Sunday when the risen Christ appears to the disciples (save Thomas, which we shall learn later) to give them the Spirit and the gift of peace. Upon receiving the gift of the Spirit, the disciples are emboldened not to preach (as Luke would have it) but to forgive sins.

Though this power to forgive sins has been traditionally understood to be the sacrament of reconciliation, this should not stop modern followers of Jesus (disciples) from forgiving others. How often do we forgive someone who has wronged us? How often do we seek forgiveness when we've wronged another? Those tasks belong to the disciples of Jesus per his handing on of the Spirit after Easter.

✦ When is the last time I forgave or asked for forgiveness?

Brief Silence

Prayer

God of mercy and forgiveness, you sent your Spirit upon your church at Pentecost to continue the ministry of Jesus to extend mercy and forgiveness to a broken world. Make us instruments of that ministry today, so that the world may be made whole by the work of that same spirit. We ask this in the name of your Son, who lives and reigns with you and the Spirit, one God forever and ever. **Amen.**

As we prepare to celebrate this feast of the Holy Trinity, let us pray for the grace to always listen to the call and counsel of God the Father, God the Son, and God the Holy Spirit . . .

Prayer

Before creation, your Spirit was there. In the fullness of time, your Word became flesh in your Son. Unite us, Father, that we may praise you above all.

Glory to the Father, the Son, and the Holy Spirit: *to God who is, who was, and who is to come.* **Amen.**

Gospel   John 16:12-15

Jesus said to his disciples: "I have much more to tell you, but you cannot bear it now. But when he comes, the Spirit of truth, he will guide you to all truth. He will not speak on his own, but he will speak what he hears, and will declare to you the things that are coming. He will glorify me, because he will take from what is mine and declare it to you. Everything that the Father has is mine; for this reason I told you that he will take from what is mine and declare it to you."

Brief Silence

For Reflection

On this feast of the Most Holy Trinity we read from the Gospel of John. Some modern readers of the New Testament are often surprised that the word "Trinity" does not appear in the Bible at all, not in the New Testament and certainly not in the Old Testament.

The term "Trinity" is a Latin-based word from *trinitas,* meaning the number three or a triad. It's a term that later Christian theologians, particularly in the patristic era, coined to talk about God, and the relationship of Father, Son, and Spirit. So, though the New Testament has many texts such as what we read today that speak of God the Father, the Son, and the Spirit, it never refers to a 'Trinity.'

This is only a four-verse passage; consider how much more there is in the New Testament! Rather than a mathematical formula to be explained and known, the Trinity is a shorthand expression for the dynamic relationship between Father, Son and Spirit. We ponder this relationship and we will never exhaust it. We drink from the wellsprings of Scripture, which never run dry.

✦ How has your understanding of the Trinity grown throughout your life?

Brief Silence

Prayer

Triune God, made known to us in the person of Jesus, the Spirit foretold his coming among us and that same Spirit remains with us today. May our lives and relationships be modeled on the trinitarian relationship of outpouring love. Give us joy in the knowledge that we are known and loved by you, triune God: Father, Son, and Spirit. **Amen.**

THE MOST HOLY BODY AND BLOOD OF CHRIST (Corpus Christi)

On this feast of Corpus Christi, we recall in a particular way Jesus' gift of his whole self to us in the Eucharist. As we begin this celebration let us pause to prepare ourselves to receive the Body and Blood of our Lord . . .

Prayer

Gracious God, you transform the humblest of our gifts into abundant and unimaginable blessing. Help us believe that, in you, we are enough.

Blood is poured and flesh is broken. *From our hearts let praises sing.* **Amen.**

Gospel   Luke 9:11b-17

Jesus spoke to the crowds about the kingdom of God, and he healed those who needed to be cured. As the day was drawing to a close, the Twelve approached him and said, "Dismiss the crowd so that they can go to the surrounding villages and farms and find lodging and provisions; for we are in a deserted place here." He said to them, "Give them some food yourselves." They replied, "Five loaves and two fish are all we have, unless we ourselves go and buy food for all these people." Now the men there numbered about five thousand. Then he said to his disciples, "Have them sit down in groups of about fifty." They did so and made them all sit down. Then taking the five loaves and the two fish, and looking up to heaven, he said the blessing over them, broke them, and gave them to the disciples to set before the crowd. They all ate and were satisfied. And when the leftover fragments were picked up, they filled twelve wicker baskets.

Brief Silence

For Reflection

The feast of the Most Holy Body and Blood of Christ has its historical roots in thirteenth-century Belgium but it is celebrated worldwide today. Our reading of the multiplication of the loaves comes from the Gospel of Luke. This episode is laden with eucharistic overtones, especially in the verbs used: taking, blessed, broke, and gave. These are the verbs used at the Last Supper, and that we use today in our eucharistic liturgy. So even though we are not reading from the Last Supper, eucharistic theology is baked into the story of the multiplication of the loaves.

It was Luke who portrayed Jesus as an infant lying in a manger (a food-trough), as food for the world. In the concluding chapter of the Gospel of Luke, on the road to Emmaus the disciples will learn that after the resurrection they come to know Jesus in the breaking of the bread. And later the apostle Paul is shown celebrating a meal with the breaking of the bread (Acts 27:35). So eucharistic theology permeates the Gospel of Luke and his Acts of the Apostles. How appropriate that we read from his gospel today, on the feast of the Body and Blood of Christ.

✦ How do you see the eucharistic pattern of taking, blessing, breaking, and giving in your own life? How have you been chosen, blessed, and shared with others?

Brief Silence

Prayer

Bread of Life and food for the world, Jesus, incarnate son of God, may we feast on you, your word, and your wisdom. You come to us daily in the Eucharist. After consuming you, may we too become bread for the world, broken and shared freely with those in need. We ask this in your holy name. **Amen.**

Jesus calls us to follow him.
For the times we have wavered in
our calling to be disciples we ask
for pardon and forgiveness . . .

Prayer

O God, your invitation to follow your Son is given to all. Increase our faith and strengthen our courage that we may not hesitate to go where he leads.

My heart is glad and my soul rejoices, *for you will show me the path of life.* **Amen.**

Gospel   Luke 9:51-62

When the days for Jesus' being taken up were fulfilled, he resolutely determined to journey to Jerusalem, and he sent messengers ahead of him. On the way they entered a Samaritan village to prepare for his reception there, but they would not welcome him because the destination of his journey was Jerusalem. When the disciples James and John saw this they asked, "Lord, do you want us to call down fire from heaven to consume them?" Jesus turned and rebuked them, and they journeyed to another village.

As they were proceeding on their journey someone said to him, "I will follow you wherever you go." Jesus answered him, "Foxes have dens and birds of the sky have nests, but the Son of Man has nowhere to rest his head."

And to another he said, "Follow me." But he replied, "Lord, let me go first and bury my father." But he answered him, "Let the dead bury their dead. But you, go and proclaim the kingdom of God." And another said, "I will follow you, Lord, but first let me say farewell to my family at home." To him Jesus said, "No one who sets a hand to the plow and looks to what was left behind is fit for the kingdom of God."

Brief Silence

For Reflection

In the gospel story today, Jesus "resolutely determined" to make his way to Jerusalem, where the reader knows what fate awaits him. There is no turning back. Three examples of "would-be disciples" illustrate the point that there is no turning back for the life of a true disciple. The first would-be disciple is told that discipleship means a life of following, without even a place to rest one's head. The second has unfinished business, the burying of the dead; yet a life of discipleship still comes first. And the third wants to say good-bye, but here, too, a life of discipleship comes first. The image is stark. Once one puts their hand to the plow there is no turning back, there is no wistful glance at what was left behind. This ideal may seem unattainable but it is the call of the disciple nevertheless. Jesus himself sets the example.

There is much to learn on the journey to Jerusalem. Luke's Jesus has many parables to teach, many examples to give, and some rebukes to issue. The conclusion of this ministry will end with the cross, the ultimate example of single-minded devotion that does not look back.

✦ Jesus gives us an example of perseverance by resolutely turning his face toward Jerusalem. What areas in your life require perseverance and determination right now?

Brief Silence

Prayer

Generous Father, you have called us on a journey to accompany your son to Jerusalem. Give us the courage and determination to be resolute, not turning back, not turning away. May we grow closer to your son on this journey, listening attentively to his teaching and following closely his way of life. We ask this in his name, for he lives and reigns with you and the Holy Spirit, one God forever and ever. **Amen.**

As modern day disciples Jesus sends us out, like the seventy-two, to proclaim the good news of God's kingdom. Let us pause for a moment to pray for the strength, humility, and grace needed to fulfill this mission . . .

Prayer

If only we believe, Lord, we can do great things in your name. Teach us to bless all people with peace and to never let disappointment discourage us from doing your will.

Let Christ's peace control our hearts, *and let Christ's word dwell in us richly.* **Amen.**

Gospel　　　　　　　　　**Luke 10:1-9 (or Luke 10:1-12, 17-20)**

At that time the Lord appointed seventy-two others whom he sent ahead of him in pairs to every town and place he intended to visit. He said to them, "The harvest is abundant but the laborers are few; so ask the master of the harvest to send out laborers for his harvest. Go on your way; behold, I am sending you like lambs among wolves. Carry no money bag, no sack, no sandals; and greet no one along the way. Into whatever house you enter, first say, 'Peace to this household.' If a peaceful person lives there, your peace will rest on him; but if not, it will return to you. Stay in the same house and eat and drink what is offered to you, for the laborer deserves his payment. Do not move about from one house to another. Whatever town you enter and they welcome you, eat what is set before you, cure the sick in it and say to them, 'The kingdom of God is at hand for you.'"

Brief Silence

For Reflection

During the ministry of Jesus there were many followers: crowds, disciples, apostles, and a special few. In the Gospel of Matthew, there are only twelve disciples, and they were also the twelve apostles (Matt 10:1-2). But Luke has a much more expansive view of discipleship. In fact, in Acts, he invents a feminine form of the word to mention Tabitha, a female disciple (9:36). And in today's gospel we have the mission of the seventy-two! Aside from this story in Luke we never hear about the seventy-two again.

And this simple lesson may give us hope today. According to Luke, men, women, the Twelve, the disciples, the seventy-two and many more were in a special relationship with Jesus, chosen to follow him and chosen also to be sent by him. In this gospel there were not such tight boundaries around who could or could not be a disciple. Instead, the situation seems to have been more fluid or dynamic. And that's likely a more accurate reflection of the situation around Jesus' earthly ministry. It would also seem to reflect our lives more accurately too, with dynamic, fluid relationships.

✦ Jesus sends the disciples out in pairs. Do you have a companion on the journey of faith? How does it change ministry when it is done in a team setting?

Brief Silence

Prayer

Lord Jesus, you called disciples during your time on earth and you continue to call disciples today. Give us an attentive spirit to hear your voice, so we may move from the margins to the inner circle, from the crowds seeking wonders to the disciples seeking wisdom. We ask this in your name. **Amen.**

In today's gospel Jesus lifts up the example of the Samaritan who acts with mercy and commands us to "Go and do likewise." Let us pause to remember the times we have not treated others as neighbor . . .

Prayer

Gracious God, in Jesus, you show us who our neighbor is. Yet we often try to limit your mercy. Teach us to love you fully by loving our neighbor as ourselves.

I will praise the name of God in song, *and I will glorify God with thanksgiving.* **Amen.**

Gospel   Luke 10:25-37

There was a scholar of the law who stood up to test Jesus and said, "Teacher, what must I do to inherit eternal life?" Jesus said to him, "What is written in the law? How do you read it?" He said in reply, *"You shall love the Lord, your God, with all your heart, with all your being, with all your strength, and with all your mind, and your neighbor as yourself."* He replied to him, "You have answered correctly; do this and you will live."

But because he wished to justify himself, he said to Jesus, "And who is my neighbor?" Jesus replied, "A man fell victim to robbers as he went down from Jerusalem to Jericho. They stripped and beat him and went off leaving him half-dead. A priest happened to be going down that road, but when he saw him, he passed by on the opposite side. Likewise a Levite came to the place, and when he saw him, he passed by on the opposite side. But a Samaritan traveler who came upon him was moved with compassion at the sight. He approached the victim, poured oil and wine over his wounds and bandaged them. Then he lifted him up on his own animal, took him to an inn, and cared for him. The next day he took out two silver coins and gave them to the innkeeper with the instruction, 'Take care of him. If you spend more than what I have given you, I shall repay you on my way back.' Which of these three, in your opinion, was neighbor to the robbers' victim?" He answered, "The one who treated him with mercy." Jesus said to him, "Go and do likewise."

Brief Silence

For Reflection

Luke tells us that a certain scholar wanted "to justify himself" and so to clarify who is his neighbor. Rather than answer straightforwardly, Jesus poses a story with which we are familiar. Though the question is about "neighbor," mercy is the keyword in this gospel. The scholar was likely predisposed to believe that the priest or the Levite would be a neighbor, by acting mercifully. But it was the person the scholar did not expect who acted in that way.

When the scholar asks, "And who is my neighbor?" the answer could rightfully be said, "The one who treated him with mercy." When one is in the ditch needing help, who is neighbor? More important than role or station, privilege or power, is the capacity and the willingness to be merciful and to receive mercy. Without mercy, the person in the ditch dies. Those who act in this way are neighbor, much more so than those we might otherwise expect. As Jesus continues to do, he creates upheaval in our worldview by a simple story that causes us to reconsider our priorities and prejudices.

✦ The man in the ditch must accept the help of the Samaritan in order to find relief. When have you received help from unexpected or even shocking sources?

Brief Silence

Prayer

Jesus Christ, Good Teacher, you spoke to your disciples in parables, allowing each to determine meaning for oneself. May we have the awareness to hear your teachings with open ears, discerning your will for us in each story. In your name we pray. **Amen.**

In today's gospel Jesus gently calls Martha away from her many burdens and anxieties to encounter him with the peace and devotion of her sister Mary. For the times our burdens and anxieties have clouded us to the presence of the Lord we pause to ask for forgiveness . . .

Prayer

O God, you send us angels in disguise, yet anxiety distracts us from seeing them. Teach us to be both Mary and Martha that we may be ready to be present to you.

Blessed are they with generous hearts, *for they shall see God.* **Amen.**

Gospel   **Luke 10:38-42**

Jesus entered a village where a woman whose name was Martha welcomed him. She had a sister named Mary who sat beside the Lord at his feet listening to him speak. Martha, burdened with much serving, came to him and said, "Lord, do you not care that my sister has left me by myself to do the serving? Tell her to help me." The Lord said to her in reply, "Martha, Martha, you are anxious and worried about many things. There is need of only one thing. Mary has chosen the better part and it will not be taken from her."

Brief Silence

For Reflection

The Martha and Mary story in Luke is so familiar many people refer to themselves as either a "Martha," meaning they are good at or even prefer working in the kitchen, or a "Mary," meaning they do not worry about such things. Indeed this gospel has been quoted so often and used to support so many various understandings of ministry, household chores, the role of women, and more, that it is good to simply step back and read the words, or listen carefully when they are proclaimed.

Jesus tells Martha in effect that the proper service for a disciple in this situation is to listen to Jesus. It is not to fret about serving meals. Luke makes this point again in Acts of the Apostles, when the apostles are too busy serving at table to be attentive to God's word and to prayer. To free themselves up for prayer and reading the word, the apostles appoint seven to serve at table, as "deacons."

The gospel reading today is not about the role of women, or the clerical/religious state versus the laity. Instead, the story demonstrates that the proper role of a disciple is attentiveness to Jesus and his word.

✦ How might you find more time in your daily life to sit at Jesus' feet and listen?

Brief Silence

Prayer

Lord, Jesus Christ, your earthly ministry was enhanced by a network of women and men. You taught them and us that the most ideal role of a disciple is to listen to you. Give us ears to hear your voice, and the desire to make time in our day to do so, for your words are light and life. In your name we pray. **Amen.**

In today's gospel the disciples approach Jesus with a simple request, "Lord, teach us to pray." Let us pause to prepare ourselves to be present to God in prayer . . .

Prayer

God, our Father, your Son taught us to pray and to ask, for you are ever gracious and merciful. Teach us to ask for only that which is pleasing to you.

God has heard the words of my mouth. *I will give thanks to God's holy name.* **Amen.**

Gospel   **Luke 11:1-13**

Jesus was praying in a certain place, and when he had finished, one of his disciples said to him, "Lord, teach us to pray just as John taught his disciples." He said to them, "When you pray, say: / Father, hallowed be your name, / your kingdom come. / Give us each day our daily bread / and forgive us our sins / for we ourselves forgive everyone in debt to us, / and do not subject us to the final test."

And he said to them, "Suppose one of you has a friend to whom he goes at midnight and says, 'Friend, lend me three loaves of bread, for a friend of mine has arrived at my house from a journey and I have nothing to offer him,' and he says in reply from within, 'Do not bother me; the door has already been locked and my children and I are already in bed. I cannot get up to give you anything.' I tell you, if he does not get up to give the visitor the loaves because of their friendship, he will get up to give him whatever he needs because of his persistence.

"And I tell you, ask and you will receive; seek and you will find; knock and the door will be opened to you. For everyone who asks, receives; and the one who seeks, finds; and to the one who knocks, the door will be opened. What father among you would hand his son a snake when he asks for a fish? Or hand him a scorpion when he asks for an egg? If you then, who are wicked, know how to give good gifts to your children, how much more will the Father in heaven give the Holy Spirit to those who ask him?"

Brief Silence

For Reflection

The Our Father prayer is something we likely learned as children, perhaps one of the first memorized or rote prayers we acquired. So, today's gospel and its version of the prayer might strike us as a bit odd. It's not the version we find in Matthew, which is much closer to the version we have memorized and recite at Mass. Instead, Luke's version has some elements that might be closer to the words uttered by Jesus himself.

This short prayer of Jesus addressed directly to the Father likely offended sensibilities of the time. This was not the mere recitation of a psalm; this was not a lengthy sacrifice of praise and thanksgiving; this was not rooted in prophets, Moses, or the Law. This was the prayer of Jesus given to his disciples.

Next time we rush through this memorized prayer at Mass or another occasion, it might be good to set ourselves in the context of Jesus and his disciples, imagining receiving this prayer and his instruction. The prayer constitutes a way of life and disposition much deeper than mere prattle.

✦ In today's gospel we are given the beginnings of the Our Father, our most treasured prayer. Say the Our Father slowly. Which line stands out to you? Why?

Brief Silence

Prayer

Jesus, our brother, son of the Father, you taught us to pray in a way that unites us all as God's children. Ever mindful of our identity, give us a spirit of reverence for all members of God's family. United in love may we serve one another as you served those you encountered. We ask this in your name. **Amen.**

In today's gospel Jesus counsels, "Take care to guard against all greed, for though one may be rich, one's life does not consist of possessions." For the times we have prioritized wealth, power, and possessions over the kingdom of God, let us pause to ask for pardon and mercy . . .

Prayer

Merciful God, from your hand we receive everything that is good. Teach us to number our days rightly that we may treasure what is precious in your sight.

At dawn, God's kindness shines forth. *Let us shout with joy and gladness all our days.* **Amen.**

Gospel   Luke 12:13-21

Someone in the crowd said to Jesus, "Teacher, tell my brother to share the inheritance with me." He replied to him, "Friend, who appointed me as your judge and arbitrator?" Then he said to the crowd, "Take care to guard against all greed, for though one may be rich, one's life does not consist of possessions."

Then he told them a parable. "There was a rich man whose land produced a bountiful harvest. He asked himself, 'What shall I do, for I do not have space to store my harvest?' And he said, 'This is what I shall do: I shall tear down my barns and build larger ones. There I shall store all my grain and other goods and I shall say to myself, "Now as for you, you have so many good things stored up for many years, rest, eat, drink, be merry!"' But God said to him, 'You fool, this night your life will be demanded of you; and the things you have prepared, to whom will they belong?' Thus will it be for all who store up treasure for themselves but are not rich in what matters to God."

Brief Silence

For Reflection

Many of us know and are familiar with Jesus' teachings. Today we're reminded that he often addressed the topic of money and the right use of it. The first story is about someone who wants his share of the inheritance. Rather than get in the middle of that quagmire (Jesus seems to have been wise not to step into that battle!), he gives a quick aphorism that's appropriate for Christian and non-Christian alike, "[O]ne's life does not consist of possessions." In fact, this teaching reflects certain schools of Greek philosophy, and even modern common sense.

The second story is called the parable of the rich fool. It is clear that bountiful harvests, storehouses, and great material blessings are not what matters to God. The parable calls us to reconsider our own harvests and storehouses. What are we acquiring and for what purpose? "[O]ne's life does not consist of possessions." It's a lesson so clear and fundamental that we need to be reminded of it again and again. Our money says a great deal about us as human beings. Our values, priorities, and interests are all expressed by the way we spend money.

✦ Our finances can tell us a lot about our priorities in life. When you look at your monthly expenses is your spending in line with what is most important to you? What about what is most important to Jesus?

Brief Silence

Prayer

O God, giver of all good gifts, we come before you mindful that all we have is from you. When we are taken with our own hubris and pride, thinking we deserve what we have, remind us that we are merely your servants. May we build up treasure in heaven rather than that which is passing here on earth. We humbly pray. **Amen.**

Jesus counsels us, "be prepared, for at an hour you do not expect, the Son of Man will come." Let us pause to prepare our hearts and minds to welcome Jesus . . .

Prayer

Lord, our God, you have entrusted us with your Son's mission to announce the Gospel to all the earth. Help us always be ready to proclaim it with our lives.

May your kindness, O God, be upon us *for we have placed our hope in you.* **Amen.**

Gospel   Luke 12:35-40 (or Luke 12:32-48)

Jesus said to his disciples: "Gird your loins and light your lamps and be like servants who await their master's return from a wedding, ready to open immediately when he comes and knocks. Blessed are those servants whom the master finds vigilant on his arrival. Amen, I say to you, he will gird himself, have them recline at table, and proceed to wait on them. And should he come in the second or third watch and find them prepared in this way, blessed are those servants. Be sure of this: if the master of the house had known the hour when the thief was coming, he would not have let his house be broken into. You also must be prepared, for at an hour you do not expect, the Son of Man will come."

Brief Silence

For Reflection

As we continue our Ordinary Time journey with Jesus to Jerusalem we hear more parables and teachings, laden with ancient imagery. "Gird your loins," has the sense of "brace yourself." It literally means something like, "tighten your pants." That image, coupled with "light your lamps" and "be like servants who await their master's return," and even "recline at table" tells us we are in the ancient world, in a culture quite removed from our own. But despite these images and the imaginary cultural bridge we must cross, we can certainly gain a sense of what is meant by these teachings. Some simply prefer to focus on the line, "be prepared, for at an hour you do not expect, / the Son of Man will come," shedding all ancient and other imagery.

When we reduce the teaching to this essential element, it becomes easier to grasp the message, which is not solely about the end times. Instead, the exhortation to be prepared applies to each of us as we do not know the time, place or date of our personal end. In other words, we don't know when we will die. And for that we should be prepared spiritually.

✦ Jesus tells us, "Gird your loins and light your lamps." How might we spiritually respond to these commands?

Brief Silence

Prayer

Jesus, Son of Man, you will come like a thief in the night, at a time we know not. May we be prepared for your arrival, having placed our priorities in line with yours. Inspire us with your values rather than the values of the world, so that we may be found ready for your coming, whenever that might be. We ask this in your name. **Amen.**

On this feast of the Assumption we celebrate the life and death of Mary, the Mother of God and her assumption, body and soul, into heaven. Let us pause, to ask that we might also completely give our lives to God . . .

Prayer

O God, in Mary, you reveal what is promised to all your people. Clothe us with the splendor of her faithfulness that we may enter your royal courts with gladness.

My soul proclaims the greatness of the Lord. *With the choirs of angels, let us sing God's praise.* **Amen.**

Gospel   **Luke 1:39-56**

Mary set out and traveled to the hill country in haste to a town of Judah, where she entered the house of Zechariah and greeted Elizabeth. When Elizabeth heard Mary's greeting, the infant leaped in her womb, and Elizabeth, filled with the Holy Spirit, cried out in a loud voice and said, "Blessed are you among women, and blessed is the fruit of your womb. And how does this happen to me, that the mother of my Lord should come to me? For at the moment the sound of your greeting reached my ears, the infant in my womb leaped for joy. Blessed are you who believed that what was spoken to you by the Lord would be fulfilled."

And Mary said: / "My soul proclaims the greatness of the Lord; / my spirit rejoices in God my Savior / for he has looked upon his lowly servant. / From this day all generations will call me blessed: / the Almighty has done great things for me, / and holy is his Name. / He has mercy on those who fear him / in every generation. / He has shown the strength of his arm, / and has scattered the proud in their conceit. / He has cast down the mighty from their thrones, / and has lifted up the lowly. / He has filled the hungry with good things, / and the rich he has sent away empty. / He has come to the help of his servant Israel / for he has remembered his promise of mercy, / the promise he made to our fathers, / to Abraham and his children forever."

Mary remained with her about three months and then returned to her home.

Brief Silence

For Reflection

The feast of the Assumption, like all Marian feasts, says more about Jesus than it does about Mary. With respect to the assumption, the church has long maintained, at least since the fourth century, a belief that Mary was taken up to heaven after her earthly life. The Eastern Church typically refers to this as the *dormition* (or sleeping) of Mary, expressing the belief that she did not die but slept, and then was taken up to heaven. The Roman Catholic Church refers to this as the *assumption*.

The reading that the church uses to celebrate this feast is Mary's *Magnificat*. She proclaims this upon meeting her sister Elizabeth. The *Magnificat* is a canticle that sets the stage for the gospel's themes. It sounds notes that will be reverberating throughout the gospel and in Acts. God lifts up the lowly and throws down the mighty. He fills the hungry with good things and turns the rich away empty. If this was Mary's theological outlook before Jesus was born, imagine the lessons he learned from her as a mother. She has been called the first disciple for good reason. The power of Christ's resurrection extended to her in life and death.

✦ Mary's canticle of praise to God reads as a manifesto on justice. How are you called to serve the God of Mary who fills the hungry and lifts up the lowly?

Brief Silence

Prayer

Jesus Christ, risen Lord, the power of your resurrection extended to your mother Mary, and extends even to us. Filled with the knowledge of your promise, may we live our days confident in our relationship with you, who lives and reigns with the Father and the Holy Spirit in heaven, one God forever and ever. **Amen.**

Today Jesus proclaims, "I have come to set the earth on fire, and how I wish it were already blazing!" For the times we have failed to burn with the brilliance of God's love, let us ask for pardon and mercy . . .

Prayer

In our distress, you are always faithful, Lord, ready to save us from our despair. Help us to trust in you alone.

God has placed a new song in my mouth. *A hymn to our God I will always sing.* **Amen.**

Gospel   Luke 12:49-53

Jesus said to his disciples: "I have come to set the earth on fire, and how I wish it were already blazing! There is a baptism with which I must be baptized, and how great is my anguish until it is accomplished! Do you think that I have come to establish peace on the earth? No, I tell you, but rather division. From now on a house-hold of five will be divided, three against two and two against three; a father will be divided against his son and a son against his father, a mother against her daughter and a daughter against her mother, a mother-in-law against her daughter-in-law and a daughter-in-law against her mother-in-law."

Brief Silence

For Reflection

Christians are so familiar with "peace on earth" as a tagline of Christianity that today's gospel can be something of a shock to the system. The angels sang, "[P]eace to those on whom his favor rests" (Luke 2:14; NABRE). So it sounds strange today to hear Jesus saying that he is *not* bringing peace but division.

We recall that early Christians often pulled away from their non-Christian families, forming new bonds with other Christians, whom they considered a new family. Most Romans for example, considered Christians to be deluded by a Judean superstition. So given that background, the idea that Jesus brought division might be seen in a different light. The peace that the Christians experienced was with one another, not the peace the world gives. And that peace might have come at the price of family divisions among those who did not understand this new way of life.

Though we share many common elements of our faith with those who have gone before us, the divisions they experienced in the early years seem distant. Still, when we take seriously the gospel message and live it boldly, we may be shunned or avoided by those we considered friends or family.

✦ Similar to the words of Jesus in the gospel, St. Catherine of Siena is quoted as saying, "Be who God meant you to be and you will set the world on fire." How is God calling you right now to be more faithful to who you are truly meant to be?

Brief Silence

Prayer

God of Love, make us blaze with the brilliance of that same love. May this flame light the world on fire so that we become one community emboldened and animated by love. Ignited by your divine love, O Lord, we will pursue justice for all members of your family. We ask this in the name of your son, the incarnation of love in the world. **Amen.**

In today's gospel, Jesus urges us to "strive to enter through the narrow door." For the times we have chosen what is easy instead of what is right let us pause to ask for pardon and mercy . . .

Prayer

Almighty God, in Jesus you have shown us the way to salvation. Free us from worry over who will be saved that our gaze may only be fixed upon Christ.

Praise the Lord, all peoples of God. *Sing praise to God who is faithful forever.* **Amen.**

Gospel   Luke 13:22-30

Jesus passed through towns and villages, teaching as he went and making his way to Jerusalem. Someone asked him, "Lord, will only a few people be saved?" He answered them, "Strive to enter through the narrow gate, for many, I tell you, will attempt to enter but will not be strong enough. After the master of the house has arisen and locked the door, then will you stand outside knocking and saying, 'Lord, open the door for us.' He will say to you in reply, 'I do not know where you are from.' And you will say, 'We ate and drank in your company and you taught in our streets.' Then he will say to you, 'I do not know where you are from. Depart from me, all you evildoers!' And there will be wailing and grinding of teeth when you see Abraham, Isaac, and Jacob and all the prophets in the kingdom of God and you yourselves cast out. And people will come from the east and the west and from the north and the south and will recline at table in the kingdom of

God. For behold, some are last who will be first, and some are first who will be last."

Brief Silence

For Reflection

Today's gospel gives us a troubling story of those who were undoubtedly disappointed. Can we imagine standing, knocking on the door to the house only to be told by the master, "Depart from me, all you evildoers!" Yet this is precisely the story Jesus tells someone who asks whether only a few will be saved. We are thereby reminded that simply knowing the Lord is not enough to be saved. Jesus exhorts the man to enter through the narrow door. And what is more, he is advised not to wait too late, for there will come a time when the master will lock the door.

This passage and others in the gospels like it remind us of an uncomfortable, and perhaps even disappointing truth. The effective answer to the man's question about salvation is that many will attempt it but not be able. And some of those who know the Lord, who ate and drank in his company, are those who will be shut out. Such a message is far from the feel good, open wide, broad path to salvation that we might imagine. And the warning to those who know the Lord should fall squarely on us.

✦ Jesus tells the people, "Strive to enter through the narrow gate." What do you think he is referring to? Where in your life do you find the "narrow gate"?

Brief Silence

Prayer

Lord Jesus Christ, teacher of wisdom, you warn us often of the dangers of complacency. Rouse us from the slumber of mere contentment and give us a spirit of striving to do your will at all times. Show us the narrow gate by which we might enter your kingdom where we desire to be eternally, with you, the Father and the Spirit, for you reign forever and ever. **Amen.**

In today's gospel Jesus cautions, "everyone who exalts himself will be humbled, but the one who humbles himself will be exalted." Let us pause to remember the times we have sought favor in the eyes of the world and shunned the path of humility . . .

Prayer

Loving God, your goodness is shelter for those in need. Teach us to give with a humble heart that seeks nothing in return but the joy of doing your will.

Sing to God, chant praise to God's name, *for God has showered us with mercy and love.* **Amen.**

Gospel   **Luke 14:1, 7-14**

On a sabbath Jesus went to dine at the home of one of the leading Pharisees, and the people there were observing him carefully.

He told a parable to those who had been invited, noticing how they were choosing the places of honor at the table. "When you are invited by someone to a wedding banquet, do not recline at table in the place of honor. A more distinguished guest than you may have been invited by him, and the host who invited both of you may approach you and say, 'Give your place to this man,' and then you would proceed with embarrassment to take the lowest place. Rather, when you are invited, go and take the lowest place so that when the host comes to you he may say, 'My friend, move up to a higher position.' Then you will enjoy the esteem of your companions at the table. For everyone who exalts himself will be humbled, but the one who humbles himself will be exalted." Then he said to the host who invited him, "When you hold a lunch or a dinner, do not invite your friends or your brothers or your relatives or your wealthy neighbors, in case they may invite you back and you have repayment. Rather, when you hold a banquet, invite the poor, the crippled, the lame, the blind; blessed indeed will you be because of their inability to repay you. For you will be repaid at the resurrection of the righteous."

Brief Silence

For Reflection

In today's gospel Jesus is being hosted by a leading Pharisee. The first piece of advice Jesus gives is practical, reminiscent of Greek philosophers and good Jewish etiquette. In fact, it sounds much like modern day Miss Manners! The aphorism, "[E]veryone who exalts himself will be humbled, but the one who humbles himself will be exalted," will be repeated later in the gospel (Luke 18:14).

The second piece of advice culminating in a promise to be "repaid at the resurrection of the righteous" is rooted more in religious identity and a belief that there would even be a resurrection of the righteous. To receive such an invitation, Jesus implores his host to invite "the poor, the crippled, the lame, the blind." In other words, invite those people who cannot reciprocate. By so doing, God himself will reciprocate on their behalf!

So we have two lessons from today's reading: humble oneself and serve those who cannot reciprocate. There is certainly more to the entire gospel message than that, but it is an excellent place to start. Moreover, both can be done in imitation of Jesus himself, who truly humbled himself and served us, we who cannot truly reciprocate.

✦ How have you experienced Jesus' saying, "[E]veryone who exalts himself will be humbled, but the one who humbles himself will be exalted," to be true?

Brief Silence

Prayer

Jesus Christ, wise counselor and sage prophet, your words are our light and life, to whom else shall we go? When we are tempted by praise or exaltation, turn our gaze to you. Give us the desire and the commitment to serve those who cannot repay, to offer help to those who are helpless. In so doing we honor you, our teacher. **Amen.**

Today's gospel challenges us to be faithful disciples of Jesus. For the times we have put other things before our commitment to Christ let us pause to ask for pardon and mercy . . .

Prayer

Your wisdom, O God, is beyond our grasp, yet you have chosen to reveal your mystery to us in Christ. May we give all that we have to follow only him.

Shelter us in your kindness, Lord, *and prosper the work of our hands.* **Amen.**

Gospel   **Luke 14:25-33**

Great crowds were traveling with Jesus, and he turned and addressed them, "If anyone comes to me without hating his father and mother, wife and children, brothers and sisters, and even his own life, he cannot be my disciple. Whoever does not carry his own cross and come after me cannot be my disciple. Which of you wishing to construct a tower does not first sit down and calculate the cost to see if there is enough for its completion? Otherwise, after laying the foundation and finding himself unable to finish the work the onlookers should laugh at him and say, 'This one began to build but did not have the resources to finish.' Or what king marching into battle would not first sit down and decide whether with ten thousand troops he can successfully oppose another king advancing upon him with twenty thousand troops? But if not, while he is still far away, he will send a delegation to ask for peace terms. In the same way, anyone of you who does not renounce all his possessions cannot be my disciple."

Brief Silence

For Reflection

Hyperbole and exaggeration can be effective rhetorical tools. But sometimes it's easy to miss this rhetorical tool when it's on the lips of Jesus in the Scriptures. A good rule of thumb is to see how the early Christians understood a passage in question. For example, Jesus advises his listeners in another story that "if your eye causes you to sin, tear it out" (Matt 18:9; NABRE)! But early Christians did not take that literally. The passage is rhetorical hyperbole. Something similar is at work in today's gospel passage when Jesus says that no one coming to him "without hating his father and mother, / wife and children, brothers and sisters, / and even his own life" can be a disciple.

Jesus is an effective preacher: he used the rhetorical tools of hyperbole and exaggeration to make his point. This can be a challenge for us if we want to take literally each and every saying of his in the New Testament. But gratefully we are part of a long line of believers, a large family of faith. They recognized hyperbole too. In the end, what Jesus demands is a wholehearted commitment, without distraction. And that's no exaggeration.

✦ The last line of today's gospel asks us to renounce our possessions in order to be Jesus' disciples. Is there a possession that does not lead to fullness of life that God might be calling for you to renounce?

Brief Silence

Prayer

Jesus Christ, who lived among us, you know our hearts and our desires. When love of money or possessions takes hold of us, give us the courage to renounce that in service to you. May nothing stand between us and our desire to be with you. We ask this in your name. **Amen.**

In today's gospel, Jesus tells three parables of the lost being found. Let us pause to remember the times we have strayed far from God . . .

Prayer

In Christ, you have reconciled the world to yourself, O God, and given us a message of mercy. Help us to rejoice in your extravagant love for all your people.

O Lord, open my lips, *and my mouth shall proclaim your praise.* **Amen.**

Gospel   **Luke 15:1-32 (or Luke 15:1-10)**

Tax collectors and sinners were all drawing near to listen to Jesus, but the Pharisees and scribes began to complain, saying, "This man welcomes sinners and eats with them." So to them he addressed this parable. "What man among you having a hundred sheep and losing one of them would not leave the ninety-nine in the desert and go after the lost one until he finds it? And when he does find it, he sets it on his shoulders with great joy and, upon his arrival home, he calls together his friends and neighbors and says to them, 'Rejoice with me because I have found my lost sheep.' I tell you, in just the same way there will be more joy in heaven over one sinner who repents than over ninety-nine righteous people who have no need of repentance.

"Or what woman having ten coins and losing one would not light a lamp and sweep the house, searching carefully until she finds it? And when she does find it, she calls together her friends and neighbors and says to them, 'Rejoice with me because I have found the coin that I lost.' In just the same way, I tell you, there will be rejoicing among the angels of God over one sinner who repents."

Then he said, "A man had two sons, and the younger son said to his father, 'Father give me the share of your estate that should come to me.' So the father divided the property between them. After a few days, the younger son collected all his belongings and set off to a distant country where he squandered his inheritance on a life of dissipation. When he had freely spent everything, a severe famine struck that country, and he found himself in dire need. So he hired himself out to one of the local citizens who sent him to his farm to tend the swine. And he longed to eat his fill of the pods on which the swine fed, but nobody gave him any. Coming to his senses he thought, 'How many of my father's hired workers have more than enough food to eat, but here am I, dying from hunger. I shall get up and go to my father and I shall say to him, "Father, I have sinned against heaven and against you. I no longer deserve to be called your son; treat me as you would treat one of your hired workers."' So he got up and went back to his father. While he was still a long way off, his father caught sight of him, and was filled with compassion. He ran to his son, embraced him and kissed him. His son said to him, 'Father, I have sinned against heaven and against you; I no longer deserve to be called your son.' But his father ordered his servants, 'Quickly bring the finest robe and put it on him; put a ring on his finger and sandals on his feet. Take the fattened calf and slaughter it. Then let us celebrate with a feast, because this son of mine was dead, and has come to life again; he was lost, and has been found.' Then the celebration began. Now the older son had been out in the field and, on his way back, as he neared the house, he heard the sound of music and dancing. He called one of the servants and asked what this might mean. The servant said to him, 'Your brother has returned and your father has slaughtered the fattened calf because he has him back safe and sound.' He became angry, and when he refused to enter the house, his father came out and pleaded with him. He said to his father in reply, 'Look, all these years I served you and not once did I disobey your orders; yet you never gave me even a young goat to feast on with my friends. But when your son returns, who swallowed up your property with prostitutes, for him you slaughter the fattened calf.' He said to him, 'My son, you are here with me always; everything I have is yours. But now we must celebrate and rejoice, because your brother was dead and has come to life again; he was lost and has been found.'"

Brief Silence

For Reflection

Our reading today is one of the most memorable of Jesus' parables. Since the story is a parable, it has many possible meanings. But one meaning which would have been clear to the early Christians is that the two sons can represent Gentiles and Jews. The younger son, the one who spends his share of the inheritance on wanton living, is representative of the Gentiles for it reflects the attitudes that many Jews had of the Gentiles of the day.

On the other hand, the Jews had Mosaic Law, which, in the parable, could be said to be the wishes of the father or God the Father. They kept the Mosaic Law and served God for many years without disobeying, as the parable indicates. But God rejoices when the hedonistic Gentile repents while offering nothing more for the observant Jews?

The moral of the story tells us about God's mercy, which does not follow strict justice. The love, care, and concern that our Father shows for his creation is superabundant. How do we react when faced with this overwhelming generosity?

✦ In the parable of the Prodigal Son, which character do you empathize with the most: the younger son who returns, the father who waits, or the older son outside the celebration? What is the message for you today in this parable?

Brief Silence

Prayer

God of mercy and loving kindness, you shower us with blessings beyond our imaginations. When we become haughty or look with pride on the gifts given to us by you, remind us that we are your servants, meant to be your actors in the world. Use us to meet the needs of the lowly and the poor. Allow your generosity to inspire us to be generous too. **Amen.**

In today's gospel Jesus exhorts us, "No servant can serve two masters." For the times we have placed other interests above God let us pause to ask forgiveness . . .

Prayer

Because of love for us, O God, your Son became poor that we might become rich. Teach us to serve him alone that we might gain the treasure of being his disciples.

Blessed be the name of the Lord *both now and forever.* **Amen.**

Gospel
Luke 16:1-13 (or Luke 16:10-13)

Jesus said to his disciples, "A rich man had a steward who was reported to him for squandering his property. He summoned him and said, 'What is this I hear about you? Prepare a full account of your stewardship, because you can no longer be my steward.' The steward said to himself, 'What shall I do, now that my master is taking the position of steward away from me? I am not strong enough to dig and I am ashamed to beg. I know what I shall do so that, when I am removed from the stewardship, they may welcome me into their homes.' He called in his master's debtors one by one. To the first he said, 'How much do you owe my master?' He replied, 'One hundred measures of olive oil.' He said to him, 'Here is your promissory note. Sit down and quickly write one for fifty.' Then to another the steward said, 'And you, how much do you owe?' He replied, 'One hundred kors of wheat.' The steward said to him, 'Here is your promissory note; write one for eighty.' And the master commended that dishonest steward for acting prudently.

"For the children of this world are more prudent in dealing with their own generation than are the children of light. I tell you, make friends for yourselves with dishonest wealth, so that when it fails, you will be welcomed into eternal dwellings. The person who is trustworthy in very small matters is also trustworthy in great ones; and the person who is dishonest in very small matters is also dishonest in great ones. If, therefore, you are not trustworthy with dishonest wealth, who will trust you with true wealth? If you are not trustworthy with what belongs to another, who will give you what is yours? No servant can serve two masters. He will either hate one and love the other, or be devoted to one and despise the other. You cannot serve both God and mammon."

Brief Silence

For Reflection

Jesus has more to say about money and how we use it than nearly any other ethical or moral matter in the gospels. And Luke the evangelist gives us more of these sayings, parables, and teachings than any other evangelist.

Today's parable has puzzled interpreters for centuries. Though the steward is being released from his position due to some dishonesty, he now acts in a shrewd way to leverage his remaining resources. He understands quickly that the money in the ledger due to him is better utilized currying favor than being handed over to the master. The master, upon realizing this, does not condemn him for stealing, for after all he was not stealing, instead, the master admires him.

We are advised to be as cunning and creative as this steward. Rather than a quick, easy read it's important to understand something of the context of the ancient world so as to more appropriately apply its lesson. It would be a misreading and a sure misunderstanding to imagine Jesus is encouraging dishonesty. Instead, with our own resources we are to be creative, using wealth for a greater good.

✦ Jesus tells us that a servant can only serve one master. In our culture what other "masters" demand to be served? How do you keep your focus on God?

Brief Silence

TWENTY-FIFTH SUNDAY IN ORDINARY TIME

Prayer

Lord Jesus, your teachings are filled with wisdom and challenge. Often you challenge us about the right use of money. Give us the insight to recognize that what we have is yours, given to us for a short period of time, and that it will remain when we go to be with you forever. May our only master be you. **Amen.**

Today Jesus tells us the parable of the rich man and Lazarus. For the times we have ignored the hungry and destitute at our door, let us pause to ask for mercy and forgiveness . . .

Prayer

O God, you have given us poor Lazarus to teach us your mercy. May we never turn away from our sisters and brothers in need for in Christ, they will lead us to your heavenly home.

Praise the Lord, my soul! *Let all my breath praise God who saves.* **Amen.**

Gospel   Luke 16:19-31

Jesus said to the Pharisees: "There was a rich man who dressed in purple garments and fine linen and dined sumptuously each day. And lying at his door was a poor man named Lazarus, covered with sores, who would gladly have eaten his fill of the scraps that fell from the rich man's table. Dogs even used to come and lick his sores. When the poor man died, he was carried away by angels to the bosom of Abraham. The rich man also died and was buried, and from the netherworld, where he was in torment, he raised his eyes and saw Abraham far off and Lazarus at his side. And he cried out, 'Father Abraham, have pity on me. Send Lazarus to dip the tip of his finger in water and cool my tongue for I am suffering torment in these flames.' Abraham replied, 'My child, remember that you received what was good during your lifetime while Lazarus likewise received what was bad; but now he is comforted here, whereas you are tormented. Moreover, between us and you a great chasm is established to prevent anyone from crossing who might wish to go from our side to yours or from your side to ours.'

He said, 'Then I beg you, father, send him to my father's house, for I have five brothers, so that he may warn them, lest they too come to this place of torment.' But Abraham replied, 'They have Moses and the prophets. Let them listen to them.' He said, 'Oh no, father Abraham, but if someone from the dead goes to them, they will repent.' Then Abraham said, 'If they will not listen to Moses and the prophets, neither will they be persuaded if someone should rise from the dead.'"

Brief Silence

For Reflection

We should find today's story of the Rich Man and Lazarus troubling for a number of reasons, not least of which is that those of us in the developed world are likely the rich man, dressed in fine clothes and eating well while there is a Lazarus effectively at our doorstep who needs our help. When examined from a global perspective, most human beings live on meager amounts each day. Most of the wealth in the world has been localized, and even if we are not part of the infamous "1 percent" we are likely among the top 25 percent globally. Indeed the annual median wage globally is about $10,000. So if we are looking to place ourselves in this parable, the person of the rich man is likely where we belong, generally enjoying the good things of this world while others go without, or go with less. The line on Abraham's lips sounds the toll of doom: "My child, remember that you received what was good during your lifetime while Lazarus likewise received what was bad; but now he is comforted here, whereas you are tormented." A reversal is in order!

✦ In his apostolic exhortation, *Evangelii Gaudium*, Pope Francis states we must allow ourselves to be "evangelized" by the poor. Have you experienced this type of evangelization in your own life? How might you open yourself up to this experience?

Brief Silence

Prayer

Jesus Christ, teacher of parables, your wisdom comes to us often in stories. Those on the margins of society, as you yourself were, have much to teach us. Give us the wisdom to go to the margins with a spirit of openness and readiness to learn. Rather than 'the privileged with the answers' may we be humble and prepared to absorb the wisdom you have prepared for us. In your name we pray. **Amen.**

In today's gospel the disciples come to Jesus with a request, "Increase our faith." Let us echo this prayer of the disciples as we pause to remember the times our faith has failed us . . .

Prayer

O God, you did not give us a spirit of cowardice but one that can do great things if we have faith. Increase our faith that we may do what you command.

Come, let us sing joyfully to the Lord; *let us acclaim the Rock of our salvation.* **Amen.**

Gospel   Luke 17:5-10

The apostles said to the Lord, "Increase our faith." The Lord replied, "If you have faith the size of a mustard seed, you would say to this mulberry tree, 'Be uprooted and planted in the sea,' and it would obey you.

"Who among you would say to your servant who has just come in from plowing or tending sheep in the field, 'Come here immediately and take your place at table'? Would he not rather say to him, 'Prepare something for me to eat. Put on your apron and wait on me while I eat and drink. You may eat and drink when I am finished'? Is he grateful to that servant because he did what was commanded? So should it be with you. When you have done all you have been commanded, say, 'We are unprofitable servants; we have done what we were obliged to do.'"

Brief Silence

For Reflection

The disciples have a simple request of Jesus today: "Increase our faith." How many of us have made the same request? In another example of hyperbole, Jesus responds by saying that if their faith was the size of a mustard seed (about the size of a sesame seed) they would be able to move trees. Now nobody, not even Jesus, moved trees. Significantly, there are other gospels where the claim is that they could with faith the size of a mustard seed move *mountains* (Mark 11:23; Matt 17:20). But apparently Luke thought that was hyperbole taken too far. For in this gospel the extent of faith is only moving trees. Mountains are not mentioned. Nevertheless, the point is simply that they have little faith, not even that the size of a mustard seed.

Jesus continues his lesson with a demonstration of the proper attitude of a servant who does what he is told expecting nothing, not even gratitude, in return. That attitude, striking for us today, is proper for discipleship. So the disciples' query about increasing their faith brings a mild rebuke from Jesus, stating that their faith is smaller than the size of a mustard seed.

✦ The disciples implore Jesus, "Increase our faith." If faith is "the realization of what is hoped for and evidence of things not seen" (Heb 11:1), what is it that you are hoping for? What unseen realities are you convinced of being true?

Brief Silence

Prayer

Father of us all, you give faith as a gift not to those who deserve or ask, but to those to whom you will. Your ways are inscrutable and beyond human comprehension. Still we ask as the disciples asked Jesus, to increase our faith. In our journey on earth we seek to comprehend you and know you more intimately, to behold the mystery that is you. In your son, whom you sent to live among us as a model of faith, we pray. **Amen.**

In today's gospel ten lepers cry out to Jesus, "Jesus, Master! Have pity on us!" Let us pause for a moment to bring our own brokenness before the Lord and to ask for mercy and healing . . .

Prayer

Your hand, O God, is always open to give blessing upon blessing without measure. May we live each day with joyful gratitude in our hearts.

In all things, let us ever give thanks, *for this is the will of God for us in Christ Jesus.* **Amen.**

Gospel   Luke 17:11-19

As Jesus continued his journey to Jerusalem, he traveled through Samaria and Galilee. As he was entering a village, ten lepers met him. They stood at a distance from him and raised their voices, saying, "Jesus, Master! Have pity on us!" And when he saw them, he said, "Go show yourselves to the priests." As they were going they were cleansed. And one of them, realizing he had been healed, returned, glorifying God in a loud voice; and he fell at the feet of Jesus and thanked him. He was a Samaritan. Jesus said in reply, "Ten were cleansed, were they not? Where are the other nine? Has none but this foreigner returned to give thanks to God?" Then he said to him, "Stand up and go; your faith has saved you."

Brief Silence

For Reflection

Today Luke reminds us that Jesus is continuing his long journey to Jerusalem, now through Samaria and Galilee. We recall that Jesus is a Galilean for whom the Samaritans were considered foreigners. The most famous Samaritan is probably the character in one of Jesus' parables known as the Good Samaritan, who offers care and comfort to the man left for dead in the ditch. That such mercy and kindness were performed by a foreigner rather than a priest or Levite would have been shocking. Today we have not a fictional Samaritan but a Samaritan leper who interacted with Jesus, along with nine other lepers.

Of course, the challenge is that the Samaritan was the only one of the ten who, upon being healed, went back to thank Jesus. Jesus himself seems to be surprised that no one but the foreigner, the Samaritan, expressed gratitude. Then, the Samaritan is sent on his way with the knowledge that his faith saved him. Even Jesus could be surprised. And even Jesus appreciated a word of thanks. Today let's make a point to express thanks to someone, cultivating an "attitude of gratitude."

✦ How do you practice an "attitude of gratitude" in your daily life?

Brief Silence

Prayer

Jesus! Master! Have pity on us! We echo the cries of the lepers for we are spiritual lepers ourselves. We seek and require your pity. We call upon you with cries of mercy. Look to us with compassion, granting your mercy to us. When, upon receiving this free gift from you, we will be filled with gratitude, sharing the abundant joy that can only be had by knowing you. We ask this in your name. **Amen.**

In today's gospel Jesus calls us to persevere in prayer. Confident in God's mercy, let us lift up the broken places in our lives and ask for forgiveness and healing . . .

Prayer

Your word, O God, is living and effective. Strengthen our will to pray without becoming weary for your loving eye never sleeps nor slumbers.

Our help comes from the Lord, *who made heaven and earth.* **Amen.**

Gospel   **Luke 18:1-8**

Jesus told his disciples a parable about the necessity for them to pray always without becoming weary. He said, "There was a judge in a certain town who neither feared God nor respected any human being. And a widow in that town used to come to him and say, 'Render a just decision for me against my adversary.' For a long time the judge was unwilling, but eventually he thought, 'While it is true that I neither fear God nor respect any human being, because this widow keeps bothering me I shall deliver a just decision for her lest she finally come and strike me.'" The Lord said, "Pay attention to what the dishonest judge says. Will not God then secure the rights of his chosen ones who call out to him day and night? Will he be slow to answer them? I tell you, he will see to it that justice is done for them speedily. But when the Son of Man comes, will he find faith on earth?"

Brief Silence

For Reflection

In today's parable, the judge is named "unjust." He is willing to (and likely has) perverted justice in cases before him, which is a clear violation of Mosaic Law. The point of naming him as an unjust judge is to make clear that his decision is for sale, whether to the widow (who likely has little money) or to her adversary. The judge is willing to make a decision in her favor simply to get rid of her, regardless of the merits of the case.

If an unjust judge is willing to do what is right simply to get rid of a persistent nag how much more will a loving Father in heaven do what is right? This simple but profound insight forms the core of the message today.

Then, the gospel ends on a puzzling note, "But when the Son of Man comes, will he find faith on earth?" The story opens with the necessity to pray always, but concludes with a question about faith. Will it be that the disciples have effectively abandoned the injunction to pray always and thereby lost their faith? This question, pertinent as it was nearly two thousand years ago, is applicable still.

✦ The gospel writer tells us the moral being illustrated in today's parable: we are to "pray always without becoming weary." How do you follow Jesus' command to pray always?

Brief Silence

Prayer

Lord and God, giver of the word, we come before you humbly, aware of our own shortcomings and our limited time on earth. Our prayer is an expression of our desire to communicate with you. We long for a deep and abiding relationship with your son, the incarnate word. Grant us the courage and wisdom to be prepared for his coming, so that we may be found faith-filled and ready. We ask this in his holy name, for he lives and reigns with you and the Holy Spirit, one God forever and ever. **Amen.**

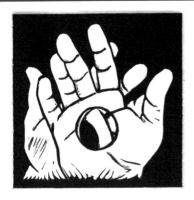

In the gospel parable of the Pharisee and the tax collector, the Pharisee is too focused on his own merits to accept God's mercy. For the times that pride has separated us from the love of God let us pause to ask for pardon and forgiveness . . .

Prayer

You, O Lord, are a God of justice, slow to anger and rich in kindness. O God, be merciful to us sinners.

I will bless the Lord at all times; *God's praise shall ever be in my mouth.* **Amen.**

Gospel   Luke 18:9-14

Jesus addressed this parable to those who were convinced of their own righteousness and despised everyone else. "Two people went up to the temple area to pray; one was a Pharisee and the other was a tax collector. The Pharisee took up his position and spoke this prayer to himself, 'O God, I thank you that I am not like the rest of humanity—greedy, dishonest, adulterous—or even like this tax collector. I fast twice a week, and I pay tithes on my whole income.' But the tax collector stood off at a distance and would not even raise his eyes to heaven but beat his breast and prayed, 'O God, be merciful to me a sinner.' I tell you, the latter went home justified, not the former; for whoever exalts himself will be humbled, and the one who humbles himself will be exalted."

Brief Silence

For Reflection

The parable today strikes one's conscience with the desire most if not all Christians have to "be right with God." This desire animated the Jewish people of Jesus' time too, and it continues to be a goal of many religious people regardless of faith or denomination. But Jesus' parable penetrates deeply into the attitudes that often lie below the surface. And for the Pharisee in the parable, his attitudes were on full display. He prays in thanksgiving that he is not like "the rest of humanity" (quite a broad stroke!) or "even like this tax collector." The Pharisee has justified himself before God by following the rules, obeying Mosaic Law, doing "what God wants" as he understands it. On the other hand, the tax collector approaches God with sincere humility, admitting his sinfulness. For that, he, rather than the Pharisee, is justified, or "right with God."

Only by acknowledging our own shortfalls without excuse and by simply relying on the mercy of God will we be placed upright before God. There is a reversal at work as the concluding line of the gospel indicates: "whoever exalts himself will be humbled, and the one who humbles himself will be exalted."

✦ If Jesus were to tell the parable of the Pharisee and the Tax Collector in your community, which characters would he use to illustrate his point about the humble and the proud? Who is given spiritual status in your community and who is looked down on?

Brief Silence

Prayer

O Lord God of justice and righteousness, we desire to be in a right relationship with you. Overlook our poor attempts at earning your favor and allow us to rest assured knowing that we have been chosen by you. Once confident of this love we will go forth to be your servants in the world, serving the poor and downcast, instruments of your mercy in our day. We ask this in the name of our Lord. **Amen.**

In the waters of Baptism we have been washed clean and sealed as Christ's own. May this water remind us of our blessedness and inspire us to follow in the footsteps of the saints . . .

Prayer

In your love, you have made us your children, O God, and counted us among your saints in heaven. May we rejoice with them and sing your praise always.

Let us seek the face of the God of Jacob, *and give praise in God's holy temple.* **Amen.**

Gospel **Matt 5:1-12a**

When Jesus saw the crowds, he went up the mountain, and after he had sat down, his disciples came to him. He began to teach them, saying: / "Blessed are the poor in spirit, / for theirs is the Kingdom of heaven. / Blessed are they who mourn, / for they will be comforted. / Blessed are the meek, / for they will inherit the land. / Blessed are they who hunger and thirst for righteousness, / for they will be satisfied. / Blessed are the merciful, / for they will be shown mercy. / Blessed are the clean of heart, / for they will see God. / Blessed are the peacemakers, / for they will be called children of God. / Blessed are they who are persecuted for the sake of righteousness, / for theirs is the Kingdom of heaven. / Blessed are you when they insult you and persecute you and utter every kind of evil against you falsely because of me. Rejoice and be glad, for your reward will be great in heaven."

Brief Silence

For Reflection

On this feast of All Saints the church gives us the Beatitudes of the Gospel of Matthew, sometimes called a "self-portrait" of Jesus. The Beatitudes are translated into English as "Blessed" but they could just as easily be translated as "Happy" as in "Happy are the poor in spirit."

We sometimes wonder what a life of Christ would look like in a different age or culture, or from different perspectives. For this we have the saints. Each saint takes as a keynote the life and mission of Jesus, then plays this song in his or her own time and place as one expression of the Christian life. St. Francis of Assisi shows how this is done in thirteenth-century Italy. St. Ignatius of Loyola shows how this is done in Reformation Spain. Mother Teresa shows how this is done in the late twentieth century. Our task is to play this song as well in our own time and place. The example of the saints shows us what the Christian life, the self-portrait of Jesus, looks like throughout history. We have many examples. Now let's go do this ourselves, live the Beatitudes in our time and place.

✦ Which Beatitude do you find most challenging? How might you seek to live this Beatitude in your own life?

Brief Silence

Prayer

God Almighty, through all times and ages you call a people to yourself, and now we too have been called. Give us the humility to recognize that we are members of a family of faith. Many have gone before us, and many more will follow. May we have the perspective to see beyond ourselves to those who will come after us and respect the earth you have given us for a home. **Amen.**

THE COMMEMORATION OF ALL THE FAITHFUL DEPARTED (All Souls' Day)

As we gather together to commemorate the souls of all the faithful departed, let us pause to remember the times our own faith has wavered and to ask for pardon and healing . . .

Prayer

We are privileged to be called members of the family of God, and our destiny is to be together forever with one another and with the Lord.

Inspire us Lord with this eternal hope, so that when we face adversity we may persevere, *with joy and love always.* **Amen.**

Gospel   **John 6:37-40 (see page 133 for other Gospel options)**

Jesus said to the crowds: "Everything that the Father gives me will come to me, and I will not reject anyone who comes to me, because I came down from heaven not to do my own will but the will of the one who sent me. And this is the will of the one who sent me, that I should not lose anything of what he gave me, but that I should raise it on the last day. For this is the will of my Father, that everyone who sees the Son and believes in him may have eternal life, and I shall raise him up on the last day."

Brief Silence

For Reflection

Yesterday we celebrated the feast of All Saints, those heroes of the faith who have gone before us as exemplars, and there are thousands! These are the ones who have been "officially" proclaimed by the church as saints. But we know there are many more saints than those. Even the apostle Paul (himself a saint) addressed his letters to the "saints" in the various locales to which he wrote. The term does not mean a "holy roller" but instead it means one who is set apart for service to God. In this latter category are likely those members of our family who have gone before us in faith, all our parents, grandparents, and even great-grandparents with all of their siblings and extended families as well may fall into this category. Christianity is a faith that is passed down through storytelling, one person telling another about what God has done in Christ. Many of these stories are in the Bible, but after two thousand years we have many more stories of heroic figures of faith to tell. And these heroes of faith extend to those we have known and loved.

✦ What is a treasured story of faith within your family?

Brief Silence

Prayer

Dear Lord, hundreds of thousands have gone before us marked by the sign of faith. We too are marked by this same sign. Give us a spirit of humility knowing that your family of faith is vast, beyond comprehension. With this knowledge may we be open to members of your family who may teach us what you have in store for us. From our parents and extended family to the countless multitudes whom we will never know. In gratitude for the grandiosity of your kingdom, we pray. **Amen.**

Other gospel options for November 2:
Matthew 5:1-12a / Matthew 11:25-30 / Matthew 25:31-46 / Luke 7:11-17 / Luke 23:44-46, 50, 52-53; 24:1-6a / Luke 24:13-16, 28-35 / John 5:24-29 / John 6:51-58 / John 11:17-27 / John 11:32-45 / John 14:1-6

In today's gospel, Zacchaeus, a tax collector and a sinner, climbs a sycamore tree so he can see Jesus. Let us pause to prepare ourselves to encounter the Lord in Word and sacrament today. . .

Prayer

To the sinner's house, you bring blessing, O God. Soften our sinful hearts with your mercy like dew, and teach us your ways of justice and love.

Every day will I bless you, Lord. *I will praise your name forever.* **Amen.**

Gospel   Luke 19:1-10

At that time, Jesus came to Jericho and intended to pass through the town. Now a man there named Zacchaeus, who was a chief tax collector and also a wealthy man, was seeking to see who Jesus was; but he could not see him because of the crowd, for he was short in stature. So he ran ahead and climbed a sycamore tree in order to see Jesus, who was about to pass that way. When he reached the place, Jesus looked up and said, "Zacchaeus, come down quickly, for today I must stay at your house." And he came down quickly and received him with joy. When they all saw this, they began to grumble, saying, "He has gone to stay at the house of a sinner." But Zacchaeus stood there and said to the Lord, "Behold, half of my possessions, Lord, I shall give to the poor, and if I have extorted anything from anyone I shall repay it four times over." And Jesus said to him, "Today salvation has come to this house because this man too is a descendant of Abraham. For the Son of Man has come to seek and to save what was lost."

Brief Silence

For Reflection

There are many parables in Luke's gospel that touch on the right use of wealth: the Prodigal Son, the Rich Man and Lazarus, the Dishonest Steward, and more. But the story of Zacchaeus is not a parable. It's about Jesus and his interaction with the wealthy tax collector. Interestingly, Jesus does not tell him to sell his possessions and give them all to the poor. That commandment is reserved for only one person, a lover of money whose sole love prevented him from following Jesus (Luke 18:18-23). No, Zacchaeus does not receive that command. He tells Jesus that he will give half of his possessions to the poor. Moreover, any extortion will be paid back four times over. With that, he is right with the Lord. So the story is about the right use of wealth, in this case, up to half of his money for the poor, making amends for any unsavory activity in his business, and paying four times anything he might have extorted.

We too can examine how we use our money, resources, and wealth. Is it for the building up of other people or for our own self-hoarding or indulgence? Our own salvation may hang in the balance.

✦ How would you answer the question, Do I serve money or does my money serve me?

Brief Silence

Prayer

Jesus Christ, you teach us many good things, among them the right use of money. In a time and place when the value of money can seem to be critically important, set our minds to you and the treasures we store up for ourselves in heaven. We ask this in your name, for you are the source of our salvation. **Amen.**

In today's gospel some Sadducees question Jesus about the resurrection. Jesus tells them God "is not God of the dead, but of the living, for to him all are alive." In thanksgiving for this gift of everlasting life, let us pause to prepare ourselves to enter into these sacred mysteries . . .

Prayer

The death of your faithful ones is precious in your sight, O God. Grant us steadfast faith that we may offer our lives to you, for resurrection is your Son's promise.

Jesus Christ is the firstborn of the dead; *to Christ be glory and power, forever.* **Amen.**

Gospel   Luke 20:27, 34-38 (or Luke 20:27-38)

Some Sadducees, those who deny that there is a resurrection, came forward.

Jesus said to them, "The children of this age marry and remarry; but those who are deemed worthy to attain to the coming age and to the resurrection of the dead neither marry nor are given in marriage. They can no longer die, for they are like angels; and they are the children of God because they are the ones who will rise. That the dead will rise even Moses made known in the passage about the bush, when he called out 'Lord,' the God of Abraham, the God of Isaac, and the God of Jacob; and he is not God of the dead, but of the living, for to him all are alive."

Brief Silence

For Reflection

Theological sophistication is on display today when Jesus responds to the derogatory question about resurrection. While Jesus is in the Jerusalem temple after making his lengthy journey, he faces a question from a powerful party of religious leaders.

This question allows Jesus the chance to correct their misunderstanding using Mosaic Law, something they would have accepted as authoritative. For him, the question was a literal understanding of resurrection to such a degree that it involved marriage in the afterlife. Jesus makes his counterargument by citing Mosaic Law and the words of Moses, who spoke of the God of Abraham, Isaac, and Jacob, all of whom died centuries before Moses. As God is the God of the living, Abraham, Isaac, and Jacob must be alive. This is a clever twist on a familiar passage, and it demonstrates the theological sophistication of this Jew from the backwaters of Galilee. He was in Jerusalem now, arguing with the learned in the temple. His audience was likely growing, and after this encounter so too was the opposition he faced.

✦ Jesus tells us in the gospel that God "is not God of the dead, but of the living, / for to him all are alive." How do you experience this in your own life of faith?

Brief Silence

Prayer

Lord God of Abraham, Isaac, and Jacob, you are the father of our Lord Jesus Christ, and you raised him from death to new life for you are the God of the living. When faced with adversity, may we be comforted with this knowledge, secure in the hope of our eternal destiny to be with you and all those we love, for we ask this in the name of that same Jesus Christ, your son our Lord, who lives and reigns with you and the Spirit, one God forever and ever. **Amen.**

As we near the end of our church year let us pause to remember the Lord's faithfulness in times of joy and times of sorrow . . .

Prayer

When darkness gathers all around us, Lord, and destruction fills our days, keep us strong in faith as we await in joyful hope for the coming of your kingdom.

With the harp and melodious song, *sing joyfully to the Lord, our God.* **Amen.**

Gospel   Luke 21:5-19

While some people were speaking about how the temple was adorned with costly stones and votive offerings, Jesus said, "All that you see here—the days will come when there will not be left a stone upon another stone that will not be thrown down."

Then they asked him, "Teacher, when will this happen? And what sign will there be when all these things are about to happen?" He answered, "See that you not be deceived, for many will come in my name, saying, 'I am he,' and 'The time has come.' Do not follow them! When you hear of wars and insurrections, do not be terrified; for such things must happen first, but it will not immediately be the end." Then he said to them, "Nation will rise against nation, and kingdom against kingdom. There will be powerful earthquakes, famines, and plagues from place to place; and awesome sights and mighty signs will come from the sky.

"Before all this happens, however, they will seize and persecute you, they will hand you over to the synagogues and to prisons, and they will have you led before kings and governors because of my name. It will lead to your giving testimony. Remember, you are not to prepare your defense beforehand, for I myself shall give you a wisdom in speaking that all your adversaries will be powerless to resist or refute. You will even be handed over by parents, brothers, relatives, and friends, and they will put some of you to death. You will be hated by all because of my name, but not a hair on your head will be destroyed. By your perseverance you will secure your lives."

Brief Silence

For Reflection

The end of the world is a popular topic among some religious people. Apocalyptic doom, fire and brimstone, death and destruction are hallmarks of the violent end of this earth by these preachers. Eschatological fervor has been with us from the time of Jesus and even before. In the decades after Jesus, many claimed to be the Messiah. Some even led certain Jews into rebellion against Rome. But Rome was decisive about striking back. Roman troops swept into Galilee and Judea to put down the rebellion, ultimately destroying Jerusalem and its temple.

Many Christians of the time considered these unfolding events a sure sign of the end times. And yet Christ's return was delayed. Luke wrote his gospel in about the 80s in part to deal with dampened and disappointed apocalyptic fervor. Christians were looking for signs that the end was near, as it had seemed to be so clear.

After centuries of such expectation, we are better off concerning ourselves with helping our neighbors, caring for the sick, and comforting the afflicted. When God himself rules, all unjust systems including war itself will end. Then we will experience an age of peace, which is good news indeed.

✦ The gospel reading ends with Jesus calling the disciples to perseverance. Where in your life are you in need of perseverance at this moment?

Brief Silence

Prayer

Lord Jesus Christ, we know not your coming and going, but we are confident of your eternal reign when we shall live in an era of peace. When the struggles of daily life afflict us, may we be strengthened by our hope in you; may we persevere in faith, knowing that you have prepared a place for us in your heavenly kingdom. We ask this in your holy name. **Amen.**

On this final Sunday of our liturgical year we celebrate the feast of Christ, the King of the Universe. Let us pause to revel in the glory of our God, and the privilege of being one of his children . . .

Prayer

Lord, on the cross, your Son showed us true power. Grant us his merciful spirit that we may be fit to share in his heavenly kingdom.

Let us go rejoicing to the house of the Lord. *Blessed be the name of the Lord, now and forever.* **Amen.**

Gospel   Luke 23:35-43

The rulers sneered at Jesus and said, "He saved others, let him save himself if he is the chosen one, the Christ of God." Even the soldiers jeered at him. As they approached to offer him wine they called out, "If you are King of the Jews, save yourself." Above him there was an inscription that read, "This is the King of the Jews."

Now one of the criminals hanging there reviled Jesus, saying, "Are you not the Christ? Save yourself and us." The other, however, rebuking him, said in reply, "Have you no fear of God, for you are subject to the same condemnation? And indeed, we have been condemned justly, for the sentence we received corresponds to our crimes, but this man has done nothing criminal." Then he said, "Jesus, remember me when you come into your kingdom." He replied to him, "Amen, I say to you, today you will be with me in Paradise."

Brief Silence

For Reflection

Today's reading tells us that Jesus was given the title "King" by Pilate, or at least by the Romans who crucified him. What is a Christian response to the Romans calling him "king" in such a mocking, derisive way? Christians embraced it and said he was king in a way unlike earthly kings, for his kingdom was not of this world. Even the thieves crucified alongside him encouraged him to save himself if he really was the Anointed One (Christ, Messiah). But again, his kingdom is not of this world. What he does have he offers the repentant thief, "[T]oday you will be with me in Paradise." The true king of a kingdom not of this world offers repentance, forgiveness, and paradise to those who seek it. The suffering encountered in this world will be reversed and overcome in the next. The one dying on a cross is destined for paradise. The authorities of this world are putting to death the king of the kingdom of God. But this king will upend the ways of the world.

We proclaim Jesus as king, the crucified humiliated one whose destiny is paradise. Let us align ourselves with him and all the poor and lowly in the world.

✦ On this feast of Christ the King of the Universe, why do you think the church would choose for us to read and meditate on Jesus' crucifixion?

Brief Silence

Prayer

Jesus Christ, King of the Universe, you are the Anointed One of God, his chosen son, sent into the world for our salvation. You were raised from the dead to new life and now you reign eternally as king. What was said in mocking derision was true. You are indeed a king. We your subjects come to you eager to enter your kingdom. Give us security and sure hope that the destiny we desire is ours. We ask this in your name. **Amen.**